Half a Millionaire

An Autobiography

by

BOB FREEMAN

Published by
A. J. Manson Ltd
Shrewsbury SY4 4SD

© 1999 by R. M. J. Freeman

All rights reserved. No part of this publication may be reproduced, stored in a retrieval system, or transmitted, in any form or by any means, electronic, mechanical, photocopying, recording or otherwise, without the prior permission of the publisher.

Published by

A. J. Manson Ltd
Shrewsbury SY4 4SD

ISBN 0 9535607 0 8

Typeset in 10/11 Times New Roman

Printed and bound in Great Britain by
Redverse Limited
Harlescott, Shrewsbury

List of Illustrations

Me (aged 9) with Ben	10
Runnis Garage	27
Venturer	29
'O'Leary's Cottage' is transformed into 'The Golden Gate'	32
'Before' and 'After' photos of the 'Quick Service Station' at Crewe	37
The 'Quick Service Station' in Hope Valley after 1954	38
'Before' and 'After' photos of the 'Oil Well' filling station at Little Compton	39
Me in my late twenties with papers relating to the Morris Agency	40
Pimley Manor from the air	45
Philip and Christopher with a repentant Sally	46
15 Mount Street	48
Stonehurst, 24 Sutton Road, which we converted into 14 flats in 1965	49
'Before' and 'After' photos of unit 86 on the Condover Industrial Estate	50
The drawing-room at Pimley Manor after restoration	54
'Before' and 'After' photos of Brooklyn House in Crewe	56
Twelve companies move into Claremont House	66
Alma House, one of the properties turned into flats by Ken Williams for Newman Associates	67
'Before' and 'After' photos of part of the Rosehill Industrial Estate	71
The Shrewsbury branch of Travelon at 25 Shoplatch	72
Me and Dorothy in 1978 with (standing between us from left to right) Christopher, Janet, John and Philip	78
'Before' and 'After' photos of Barnagearagh	83
'Before' and 'After' photos of 73 Wyle Cop	88
The Howard Street Warehouse, now the Buttermarket	89
The restored frontage of the old RSI	94 & 95

DEDICATION

*For all those who have helped
me on my way through life
and especially
for my wife*

CHAPTER ONE

The most critical event in the story I am going to tell you happened when I was thirteen years old. I kept it secret from each of my four children until they had reached the same age, considering that if I was old enough at thirteen to have done what I did, they should be old enough to understand why.

In each case, when the moment came for me to tell my secret, I felt anxious that I might go down in that child's estimation with a thump. This was because in the intervening years I had become an established member of the community, and I assumed that was how my children saw me, so they might be shocked to discover that their Dad had in fact been a rebel and not just an ordinary rebel at that! Janet, my youngest child, had thought I was so staid that she could score a major moral victory over me if she could prove that I had exceeded a thirty miles per hour speed limit by a single mph!

The ghastly secret I had to reveal was that at the age of thirteen I had run away from home, had changed my name, and had then had no contact with my Mother, sisters or step-father until I was twenty-six. I also had to explain that although I had used all my powers of persuasion to encourage my children to shine academically, I myself had pulled out of school at thirteen, and had never gone back.

So when each of my children in turn reached the appointed age and was let into my secret, it was a great relief that instead of their being shocked and filled with doubt, the reaction in each case was something like: "Good old Dad! We always thought you had an exciting story up your sleeve."

That story begins with my birth as Robin Montier Day at Plumpton in Sussex on 28 November 1928. So I am a Sagittarian; and although I don't really believe in astrology I do think that the season of the year when one enters this world may have a major influence on one's temperament. Like many Sagittarians, I was certainly born lucky.

I also believe that people tend to find what they expect to find, and that my positive outlook has helped luck to come my way. If you have a positive outlook, then all you have to do is to try to be in the right place at the right time. It works the other way too, and if you expect Doom and Disaster, then D and D is what you will probably get.

My start was not a fortunate one, either personally or in terms of the situation in the wider world. My father Geoffrey Day had been wounded in the middle of the Great War of 1914-1918, probably while fighting in the Battle of the Somme, and was already dying of cancer when I was born. He was dead before my second birthday, so sadly I have no memories of him. In the wider world, I was born in the shadow of the Great War; I was born on the verge of the Great Depression of 1929-1931; and I was still only ten years old when the Second World War broke out in September 1939.

My father's family came from Walthamstow, where his parents had owned the Ferryboat Inn. My paternal grandmother Jane Day is said to have been an extremely tough-minded lady, and the story goes that it was she who saw the opportunities stemming from the advent of commuters to that part of the world, and egged on my grandfather Harry Day and his brothers to build a substantial part of Walthamstow. Much of their work still survives; and even though I had no formal training in that sphere, building appears to have been in my blood from the beginning.

My father Geoffrey was one of three children, the others being my aunts Janet and Gladys. He had trained with Chappells as a tailor, a profession to which he returned after being invalided out of the army; but when my grandfather died he inherited enough money to set himself up as a gentleman of independent means, and he bought a five-acre property at Plumpton in Sussex (not far from Lewes) where he hoped to make his fortune by growing asparagus. Sadly in those days it took five years to get an asparagus field into maturity, and by that time he was already a dying man.

But first, in 1923, at the age of 31, Geoffrey had met and married my mother, Louise Reeve, a blue-eyed 28-year-old who in her own way was as capable and as formidable as her new mother-in-law. Louise curiously seems to have regarded my father's background as slightly inferior to her own. Her own father Gilfred Reeve was a brewer's agent: a good position, but one he hated all his life; and sadly he had died in 1918, so I would never meet him. Her mother, Alice Strange, was the daughter of Mary Montier, a Swiss girl who had efficiently swept Edward Strange off his feet when he was on a walking tour in Switzerland in the mid-1850s.

Louise herself was one of five children, the others being Montier (always known as Monty), Kathy, Mary and Louise's twin sister Clare. As a girl, Louise had idolised Monty, who had trained and qualified as an actuary. Tragically, before he could begin practising he was caught up in the Great War and was killed in action on the Western Front in 1916.

My parents spent the seven years of their marriage at Plumpton, and I believe that until my father's final illness it was a happy household. Before I appeared on the scene, Louise had given birth to my two elder sisters Diana and Janie (respectively five and three years older then me) and she appears to have entertained all our London-based relatives at weekends.

Louise was indeed a very sociable woman. Several rapturous volumes have survived of the so-called *Plumptonian Magazine* to which many of her guests contributed; and in the 1927 number there is an agreeable poem headed *The Festival of Whitsun*, written in the style of Longfellow's *Hiawatha*. It begins:

> See the merry tribes assemble
> For the Festival of Whitsun
> At the portals of Treyarnon
> At the wigwam of Louisa,
> Of Louisa the great hostess.
> On the steps she stands to greet them,
> Smiles upon them all in welcome,
> Smiles as does the sun in summer
> In the pleasant moon of Ascot...

The following year, in the 'Court and Society News' of the *Plumptonian*, under the heading 'The New Arrival', we may read that:

Much to everybody's surprise on November 28th 1928 a stork was seen to fly over Treyarnon and deposit a new male member of the P.W.E.G. On being asked his name he shouted 'Robin!' and lapsed into silence. He is already displaying all the necessary qualifications for membership in the way of cheerfulness, energy and appetite.

Incidentally, the illustrations in the *Plumptonian* were by Aunt Mary Reynolds, a talented artist who not only exhibited several times at the Royal Academy, but who also designed and painted the famous Yardley lavender trade mark.

Shortly before my father's death, we moved to Tunbridge Wells. Then we went on to Brookmans Park and finally, when I was about three-and-a-half years old, to 11a Buxton Road, Chingford. My first memories date from that time. I remember watching my two sisters go off to school, and longing to go with them. I remember racing rain drops down the window pane. I remember Sunday evenings, when we were visited by my grandmother Alice and, with Mother at the piano, we sang hymns. There was no television in those days, and we didn't have a wireless, so that Sunday evening singing was the highlight of the week especially as if I had been good I was allowed to choose one of the hymns. Grandma lived within walking distance, and I remember that she had a biscuit tin on her sideboard; but I also remember never wanting to use her toilet, because it was down a dark corridor, and in that corridor there was a reproduction of Holman Hunt's *The Light of the World* which terrified me. I also remember the horror of wash-days which came round without fail every Monday, and meant the gas boiler, skiffle rubbing-boards, Sunlight soap, Robin starch, steam everywhere and, on wet days, damp clothes hanging on clothes driers around open fires. I also remember the extent to which I was surrounded by women.

The deaths of my father, my uncle Monty and both grandfathers meant that as a comparatively tender plant I was left to the mercies of an all-powerful matriarchy. This consisted principally of my mother, my grandmother, three aunts on my mother's side of the family and two on the other, and my two elder sisters. [The fact that the aunts were all married seemed to make no difference.] There were also various cousins, several honorary aunts, sundry mother's helps and companions, and in due course two school-mistresses and a half-sister. I once tried adding them all up, and found there were at least twenty of them: a fearsome female phalanx if ever there was one.

Aunt Janet was a great character who wore fashionable 'bucket' caps. We much enjoyed visiting her in the grand house on the other side of London where she lived with her children Alan and Barbara (who had been christened Rowena, but hated the name), and her husband Cecil Shaw. Cecil was a successful engineer and businessman, who had founded Crypton and the Lancashire Dynamo Company, so they had enough money to make things happen. They even had holidays abroad, which was most uncommon in those days.

My mother would drive us there and back in our ancient Triumph 8-horse-power four-seater tourer. I remember that on our way home one day, the gear lever of our Triumph came away in Mother's hand and we ground to a halt in the middle of the highway. She dealt with this disaster by just sitting there and brandishing the offending lever above her head! Before long some Good Samaritans had obligingly pushed us to a garage, where a mechanic put us into second gear, in which we then continued home. Nowadays we would almost certainly have had to wait for a new lever costing hundred of pounds.

I was proud of our Triumph, and not long afterwards, when I had started at Mornington Road School, I did myself no good at all during a discussion of the formal Triumph held in honour of the Emperor Claudius, at which the defeated British leader

Caractacus and his family were featured in a victory parade. Feeling that I had something valuable to contribute, I put my hand up.
"Yes, Robin, what is it?" asked Miss Hunt.
"Please, Miss, my mother has a Triumph!"
Unfortunately this news did not seem to impress her a great deal.

Miss Hunt, who seemed to me to do all the work, presided over Mornington Road School in collaboration with Miss Nix, who was the more dominant of the two. Children were more innocent in those days, so we never managed to think of a suitably perverse set of rhymes for Miss Hunt; but we felt very pleased with ourselves when we chanted a rhyme which somehow associated Miss Nix with her knickers.

The three classrooms at Mornington Road were formed by the simple expedient of using two folding wooden 'walls' which ran out along grooves in the floor and ceiling to divide a single long room into three equal parts. These 'walls' were folded back for assembly each morning, when (accompanied by Miss Hunt on the piano) we sang hymns like *Onward, Christian Soldiers!* as loudly as we could. Miss Nix would then give us her orders for the day, often coupled with her standard warning about the dire misdeeds of a boy whom she somehow never needed to name.

"I know who he is!" she would declare fiercely. "And he knows who he is! He had better come to my study straight after assembly, or the consequences will be severe: not only for him, but for any of his friends who might have condoned his offence. Always assuming", she would conclude, "Always assuming that it is possible for a boy so bad to have any friends in the first place!"

Fortunately for me, I had the knack of keeping a low profile and staying out of trouble.

In later life I have become practically allergic to gardening; but while I was at Mornington Road I had a small garden in which I delighted. For some reason I stuck to potatoes, which I dug up carefully during the summer term only to replant them again.

As well as gardening, we went on nature walks, on one of which I somehow managed to strain my back. Once the problem had been diagnosed, the remedy was in no doubt. Miss Hunt and Miss Nix prescribed a warm bath in their house, which adjoined the school. They came into the bathroom and soaped my back. These days they would probably be accused of child molestation; but I think it was a delightful experience for all three of us; and it certainly cured my back.

I nearly damaged my back much more seriously the day I heard Mother talking to the milkman by the front door. I was upstairs at the time, but I liked the milkman and anyone else who was interesting and did things in the world outside my home, so I rushed towards the stairs at full speed, missed the top stair and began falling head-over-heels all the way down. As I fell, I couldn't help thinking of my favourite story, in which Christopher Robin's teddy bear, Winnie-the-Pooh, wonders whether there is any other way of coming down stairs than going bump, bump, bump. And then I heard the milkman shouting out:
'Don't worry, missus! I'll catch him!'
And luckily for me, he did.

Not long afterwards, I had to do another head-over-heels, this time as part of a family show produced by Mother. I came onto the stage with a cushion, as rehearsed, and did what was expected of me; but I must have been a perfectionist even then, because I turned crossly to my audience, called out 'Wong, wong!' and gave them a repeat performance.

In spite of my affinity with Winnie-the-Pooh — and I mean the unreconstructed Winnie-the-Pooh as portrayed in A.A.Milne's wonderful volumes, not the somewhat sugary bear of the Disney cartoon — I never owned a teddy bear myself. My own bed-time friend was a rabbit. He didn't look like a rabbit: he was red with a white shirt-front. I called him Rabbit chiefly so as to avoid any doubt on the matter. I also had a red pedal-car. There was very little scope for riding it, and it was also very decrepit, but I loved it and I was heart-broken when Mother decided that it was no longer any good, and condemned it to be buried in the garden. I sometimes wonder whether it's there still...

Red seems to have been my colour. When I decided to try my hand at painting, for example, it was with a large pot of red paint which someone had conveniently left within my reach. My aim was to improve a pair of deck chairs, also conveniently to hand. Now a number of comedians, including Norman Wisdom, have done wonderful comic routines with deck chairs. I beg to suggest that I left them all standing. However, by the end of my routine I was almost as thoroughly painted as the deck-chairs; and when my Mother saw what had happened she unaccountably seemed to regard it as more of a tragedy than a comedy.

Many people pass in and out of our lives leaving no permanent mark, and I remember nothing of our immediate neighbours in Buxton Road; but the elderly Miss Stratton from across the road remains vividly in my memory. Dressed in blue from head to foot, and with her skirt at ankle length, she swept proudly along the pavement beneath a large elaborate layer-cake of a hat, held in place by ferocious-looking hat pins. She also sported gold-rimmed glasses on a cord and a black ribbon round her neck.

I also remember some of the shop-keepers: the baker, for example, a cheerful fellow who would sell us a bag of stale buns for a penny if we were going to the zoo the next day. I was told that elephants had a particular penchant for stale buns, so if I found any that were not stale enough, I kindly saved them from any disappointment by eating the buns myself.

Then there was balding Mr. Tanner the chemist. As a sign of his trade, he had two large bottles in his window, one filled with green liquid and the other with red. Inside, his shop was fitted out in mahogany. There were dozens of mahogany drawers. On each drawer there was a white label, and on each label bold black serious lettering told of the chemical compound within. In front of the drawers was a curved glass counter-front, way above my head; and in front of that, a chair on which elderly persons could sit while Mr. Tanner mixed up potions to cure them of their ills. Mr. Tanner also sold items like soap and toothpaste; and the pink bar of scented soap which I bought from him was my first significant purchase. It was for Mother's birthday, and there was considerable mirth when I blurted out in one breath, in case she overlooked the fact, 'I bought it with my own money and I am so proud!'

McChesney's, the shop where we bought our groceries, contained not just a grocer but, as the shop-front proclaimed, 'grocers and provision merchants'. I was already learning some history in those days; and when I read the words 'provision merchants', I imagined them provisioning vast sailing ships with corned beef and ships' biscuits. I believed that Livingstone had come here (followed not long afterwards by Stanley) to fit himself out with salted provisions and whatever special things were needed to sustain explorers in darkest Africa.

Grocers in those days always wore a special white apron which came to a point, chest-high. Thus attired, Mr. McChesney reigned on his side of the mahogany counter, reaching for items from the shelves at Mother's command, or slicing quarter-pounds of ham and bacon in the monstrous red and silver hand-operated slicing machine. In front of the counter there was a vast assortment of biscuits, displayed in biscuit tins with glass lids; and the shop was filled with the delicious smell of brown sugar, dates, raisins, treacle and a thousand and one other items which were then exposed to the air instead of being tightly sealed as they are in today's supermarkets.

There were also two sweet shops: the respectable but expensive one in which anything I could afford to buy seemed to last me hardly any time at all; and the other one, frowned on my Mother, which had trays of things for a ha'penny, including sherbet, aniseed balls, sugar mice, dolly mixtures, jelly babies and gob-stoppers. As for the owner: even if (as was rumoured) her blonde hair came out of a peroxide bottle, she was kindly and had time for me.

Finally there was the shoemaker, a small rather dour man, perpetually leather-aproned and perpetually dirty, who worked on ancient machinery in the most squalid and untidy shed I had ever seen. However, not long after my fifth birthday, something the shoemaker said gave me the chance of asking whether I could help him in any way. To my intense delight — because I felt he was treating me like a grown-up — he asked me if I would like to dress his window. Soon, with a penny and a three-penny bit clutched in my fingers (there were 240 pennies to the pound in those days), I was hurrying off to the newsagents, with the responsibility not only of buying a packet of crepe paper, but of choosing the colour myself. Then I cleared and redid the window with rubber soles and heels, and pieces of leather, and tins of dubbin and boot polish. Every time I went past I checked my window display to see that it was still looking as perfect as on the day I had created it, and I glowed with happiness in the knowledge that the shoemaker was my friend, and I was his.

My world was completed by dear old Doctor Murphy and Mrs. Murphy the doctor's wife. They sound like characters from a game of 'Happy Families', and that was how they seemed. They had a bottle of medicine for every occasion, and they mixed it themselves and put it in a box in their porch. Some of it was yellow, some red and some black. I remember that black was the most repulsive of all. Even when Dr. Murphy became caught up in the vogue for removing tonsils, he made a gala of it, filling a small ward with me, my sisters and every cousin he could lay his hands on. It was great fun, and part of a world in which, despite the loss of my father, I felt secure.

Little did I know the extent to which things were about to change.

First my grandmother died; and then Thomas Francis Fox appeared on the scene. I thought of him as Brer Fox, visiting the vixen's lair; and almost before I could have said 'prickly bush' I found myself dressed up as a kind of pageboy with a brand new solid gold tie pin, and we had a wedding on our hands. My new step-father had an impeccable background, with his BSc., his war experience serving as a Second Lieutenant in army intelligence in Mesopotamia, and his career as a maths teacher at Hackney Down High School. He was also the secretary of the local tennis club and a useful bridge partner. He was also a good man; and he and my mother pecked each other on the cheek quite amicably for another 47 years. Yet after his death she told me that she had known it was a mistake from the very first week of the marriage. For one thing he was too easy-going for his own good, and soon he had allowed Mother to dominate him completely.

He also developed into the most boring conversationalist I have ever known, becoming progressively more tedious as the years went by. His sole subjects of conversation appeared to be Mesopotamia, his one holiday in Switzerland, and the boys he had taught. And from what Mother said years later, when she volunteered the opinion that 'fortunately, this sex business has never been of great importance in our family', I would guess that side of their lives was also unsatisfactory. However, in spite of this they managed to beget my beautiful red-head half-sister Margaret. So whenever I am asked "How many sisters do you have?" I am able to reply "Two-and-a-half!"

At five years old I was of course completely innocent about sexual matters. For some reason I was convinced that all dogs were male, and all cats female. I had a shrewd idea that the mystery of sex hinged on the navel, because I could not account for it in any other way. The purpose of every other part of the body seemed to be clear enough. However some passing doubts must have troubled me, because before my sixth birthday I had taken the opportunity, when on holiday, to remove the pants from a co-operative young lady. At last I knew what the difference was between the male and female body; though it would be many years before I put my new knowledge to any good use.

One advantage of Mother's second marriage was that our financial situation improved from 'struggling' to 'comfortable'. Soon a new house was being built for us on the edge of Epping Forest. As usual the foundations looked far smaller than they really were. 'Pop' (as we called our step-father), was sure that our dining table couldn't possibly fit into the space provided for the new dining-room, and it needed a tape-measure to prove him wrong.

CHAPTER TWO

In the summer of 1935, when I was six-and-a-half, we celebrated the Silver Jubilee of King George V and Queen Mary. Uncle Walter (a consulting water engineer whom Aunt Mary had married rather late in life) rented a first-floor window in a department store on the route of the procession. We had to be there very early and we stayed for the whole day, having taken sandwiches and buns, thermos flasks and lemonade. It was very exciting watching the procession going past, and hearing the cheering of the crowds down below, and Uncle Walter presented each of us with a commemorative silver medal to mark the occasion.

After this I became more aware of events in the larger world; and it was a time of many changes. By the following year, King George V was dead, and the Prince of Wales had become Edward VIII. But when the dry, stuffy Prime Minister Mr. Baldwin asked Edward to choose between the crown and his love for a divorced American woman, Wallis Simpson, he put love before duty and abdicated in favour of his brother who became George VI. All these events, including Edward's moving abdication speech, were brought to us by our new wireless set. We all started listening to the news each evening, and there was high drama in the chimes of Big Ben and the measured tones of the news-readers who, we were told, always had to wear evening dress in front of the microphone.

The wireless also brought us popular music. This was the era of the Big Bands, and each week the BBC featured a different band, so that we heard the music of Henry Hall, Joe Loss and many others. I well remember the friendly voice of Reginald Forte who played the theatre organ for us. We also had a hand-wound gramophone, on which we could play twelve-inch records which spun round at 78 revolutions per minute. At the same time my sisters, and thousands like them, bought the sheet music of numbers like *The Lambeth Walk,* and *Goodbye, Old Ship of Mine,* which could then be played on the piano at home. Sheet music cost around a shilling (a twentieth of a pound) or one shilling and sixpence — quite expensive when the average wage was no more than two pounds a week.

Outside the home, we began to be taken to the cinema, where it was a terrific thrill to see and hear a mighty Wurlitzer organ emerge majestically from the orchestra pit while being bathed in a spectrum of different colours. Cinemas had a complete programme at that time: the main feature, a secondary or 'B' movie, a quarter-of-an-hour of Movie-Tone or Pathé news, and trailers of the next week's films. I remember that the first film I ever saw was Charlie Chaplin's *Modern Times.* Curiously, although Al Jolson had introduced sound to the big screen nine years previously, Chaplin was a reluctant talker, and *Modern Times* was a silent film.

The move to our new house at Sewardstonebury was only slightly marred by the fact that, apart my other chores, I was expected to go out at frequent intervals in order to fill a bucket with stones from the new garden. I'm sure this needed doing: but there was no competitive angle, let alone any reward. It was boring and lonely work, and it felt like punishment.

In other ways the move was highly beneficial. Our garden ran down to Epping

Forest, and I was able to wander at will through the forest and across the plains. The roads were much safer then, and I cycled anywhere I wanted to go. Some of my favourite haunts were Connaught Water, where there was boating, and the swimming pool at High Beach. I also enjoyed visiting the pond for model boats at the Butler Retreat. This establishment, not far from Queen Elizabeth's Hunting Lodge, was a kind of tuck and lemonade establishment. However little money you had, there would always be something you could afford.

I sometimes went to the Butler Retreat with my cousin John Cunningham who, being two years my senior, seemed to me to be very knowledgeable and mature. One day, I remember, he announced that he had learned two new rude words. Had I any to swap with him? I had not. Despite this failing on my part, he very generously decided to tell me his two words anyway. Since they were too rude to risk anyone overhearing, he told me in a confidential whisper that they were 'cuck' and 'funt'. I was tremendously impressed though, as I later realised, none the wiser.

By this time we had acquired a new car, a 1936 Austin 10 Lichfield Saloon. It had leather upholstery, wire wheels, and solid rubber running-boards along each side of the car. The driver's intentions of going left or right were signalled by nine-inch long illuminated 'trafficators', which swung out of slots in the door pillars; and the headlamps had a remarkable arrangement which, activated by a foot switch, deflected the near-side light to the kerb while altogether extinguishing the right-hand light. It also had a manual starting-handle for use when the car wouldn't start normally. Of course there were no modern luxuries like screen-washes, car radios, or even interior heating. If the weather was cold, we simply took car rugs with us.

The principal drawback of the Austin 10 was that the only way to carry any sizeable amount of luggage was to fix the boot lid down, and strap the cases to it, because when the boot lid was closed, there was only room for the spare tyre and a tool kit. The result was that when we went on holiday we three children travelled in extreme discomfort, with large numbers of parcels and packages stuffed all round us in the back of the car.

Our first long car journey was to Dunster, not far from Blue Anchor Bay in the Bristol Channel. It was there that I learned to swim. I was particularly pleased with this accomplishment, believing that at last I had outdone my cousin John. Pride as usual came before a fall, because when we drove the three miles over to Minehead, where he and his family were holidaying, his first words were: 'I can swim!'

Back home, I would have liked to join the Scouts. Gilwell Park, home of the Scout movement, was only just up the road, and that was where the World Scout Jamboree was held. I much admired their South African style hats, and their khaki shirts covered with badges; but I was told that I was too young, and sadly no-one added that I could have started by joining the Cubs.

My most constant companion at that time was our wire-haired Terrier Ben, who always seemed to have a sympathetic ear for my problems. If there were North Poles to be reached, or Heffalumps to be hunted, he was Piglet to my Winnie-the-Pooh. As for human beings: my taste was less for relatives than for people who appeared to be doing something real in the world, such as grooms, gardeners, chauffeurs and maids. Grooms at near-by stables would allow me to help clean harnesses in the tack room,

Me (aged 9) with Ben

and then include me in orgies of bread and jam and tea. Chauffeurs would usually talk to me about their cars. And there were some lovely maids around, such as our Doris, who was young and pretty, and would have long conversations with me about her boyfriend Bill.

Relatives tended to be women, or men dominated by women. Each Christmas, for example, we went to what was always known as 'Aunt Kathy's Christmas Party'. This was despite the fact that her husband, kindly Uncle Joe, was a man of considerable importance since he ran the family estate office at Walthamstow. But the aunts continued to dominate the uncles. Take Aunt Clare, for example: her husband, Uncle Dan Cunningham, was a shipping man, and a senior manager in the Cunard line. However, when encountered in his home habitat, his only interests appeared to be growing roses and playing bridge; here at least he showed some mettle: woe betide any partner of his who failed to play their cards right — unless of course his partner was one of the aunts. As for business: I suppose these great men knew that it was of no interest to the aunts, and so it had become an unmentionable subject.

Perhaps the most independent of my uncles was Fred Dix, who had married my paternal aunt Gladys. An air of mystery clung to him, on account of his first wife having committed suicide. In addition, he was a pioneer of motor transport, who had founded the first motor charabanc service in Oundle. Aunt Glad was proud of him, and told me that he had once been the world speed skating champion. Uncle Fred was certainly special to me, because he was the first motor caravanning enthusiast I had ever met, and when I was only seven years old the two of them took me on a camping holiday in Devon. Fred treated me like an equal, and it was a very happy holiday, their good humour surviving even the thunderstorm which washed us out in the middle of the night. It was a shame that Aunt Gladys had married too late in life to have any children of her own.

But the uncle who would influence my life most strongly was my dead Uncle Monty. Mother wanted me to idolise him, just as she had done. Worse, she wanted me to follow in his footsteps and become an actuary: not because it suited my temperament or abilities, but because she wanted me to lead the life of which he had been robbed by his death in the Great War. How was I to have a life of my own?

At about that time I began to get worried about my appearance. For one thing, I was being teased about the size of my nose. It now appears to me to be a perfectly respectable nose; but in those days I was told that it wasn't a proper nose at all, that it was so small that it was not much more than the shirt-button traditionally used on rag dolls. My hair was another anxiety to me, being so wiry that neither water nor Brylcream could flatten it down enough to produce anything remotely like the regulation 'parting' at sides or front. I had certainly never seen an adult with hair like mine. Indeed I became convinced that I would grow up to be a wild-haired nose-less monster. This was particularly alarming, because my (utterly false) assumption was that growing up should be a process not just of growing larger, but of moving from imperfection to perfection. Adults, we were taught in those days, were *by definition* always right. I also decided that I didn't like my christian name. 'Robin' meant 'Robin red-breast', and was another reason for being teased.

I achieved a little more independence when I was sent to St Aubyns, a Woodford Preparatory School for boys of seven or eight to thirteen. 'Crumps', as it was affectionately known after its founder Colonel Collie, suited me very well, and I progressed fairly quickly through the school. Unfortunately the efforts of the English masters to teach me English grammar were an almost complete failure, though I did learn the difference between a noun and a verb. The French master, whose nickname was Tin-Tack because he was so sharp, was more successful, and although I had great difficulty with spoken French, I learned to cope with the written language quite well. But for me the highlight of my period at 'Crumps' was the time I spent in the carpenter's shop. The carpenter, a steady unsmiling man, was a master of his trade and an excellent teacher. He recognised and helped me to satisfy my creative streak; and some of the book-cases and cupboards I made under his direction still survive.

Occasionally I was invited out to lunch by 'Aunt' Annie, who was slim, petite, and efficient enough to see that I always got back to school on time. Honorary aunts came in all shapes and sizes; and occasionally my Mother organised a gathering she called 'the Strange muster' at which up to fifty of these curious connections would appear. It was very kind of her, but I sometimes felt that she was far more interested in other grown-ups than in us children. We weren't expected to be 'seen and not heard' as in Victorian times, but she hadn't progressed very far beyond that state of affairs, and this distanced me from her just as much as her determination that I should be an actuary.

The summer after I had learned to swim, Aunt Ethel, another honorary aunt, saved me from taking part in the swimming sports at Crumps. The point was that if you could swim at all, you were expected to take part in a swimming race, and I was dreading it. Fortunately, on sports day Aunt Ethel was staying with us; and although she was a dear old party she was also rather large and unwieldy. The problems of fitting her and everything else necessary into the car proved almost insurmountable, and by the time we reach St. Aubyn's my race was over. Although I hadn't wanted to lose face by failing to show up, it was a tremendous relief that I had survived to swim another day.

Yet another honorary aunt was Aunt Sarah Strange, who lived to be 106, and won an octogenarian prize for crochet so many times in a row that eventually, finding that everyone else was becoming too discouraged, the authorities had to persuade her to retire unbeaten. She lived in Worthing, where we children went to convalesce at the San Remo Guest House if we had suffered from one of the usual childhood illnesses such as chicken-pox or measles. Anyone who was well enough in the mornings went swimming; and if one swam (and only if one swam), one got a large 1d (one penny) currant bun.

It was during one of our stays at Worthing that we went walking on the South Downs at Washington, and Mother saw a cottage for sale. It was on offer at £400 — exactly the sum of money which she had inherited from Grandma — and she fell in love with it and bought it. It immediately became our holiday home, and although it was not very well built, had only two bedrooms and no indoor water (though there was an outdoor well and we installed the luxury of a hand-operated pump in the kitchen so that we could pump our own water), from then on the cottage probably brought her more happiness than anything else in her life.

Our new cottage was one of only four properties in the local community, which apart from ourselves consisted of the Noyces, the Fielders and Mr. Rance.

The Noyces lived next-door to us in a ramshackle elm-boarded bungalow. They were true country people whose lives centred round their kitchen. This was almost completely filled by a large wooden table groaning under the weight of bowls, buckets, cans, bottles and boxes containing all that was needed for feeding them and their considerable menagerie of animals. They kept goats, which were taken out and tethered by long chains to a different area of Downs grass each day; but the goat kids were not tethered, and seemed to delight in making as much noise as possible by finding corrugated iron roofs and then tap-dancing on them.

At first Mr. Noyce was a mystery to me. I never saw him on horse-back, yet he always wore riding-breeches, brown boots and brown leather gaiters, topped by a collarless shirt and a tweed jacket. He seemed extremely nimble, yet I met him coming back from his walks with an old man's walking stick. Nor did I connect his absences with the occasional sound of a gunshot. However the day came when I caught him virtually red-handed, and he then showed me that his 'stick' had a concealed trigger, with a removable stock, and a ferrule hiding the business end of the barrel. As for his tweed jacket: it had accommodatingly large game-keeper's or rather poacher's pockets.

Mr. Fielder had some success as a speculative builder, and he and his wife were happy-go-lucky folk. He once asked Mother if I could help him round up some chickens. She agreed, and I went out for what turned out to be an outstandingly enjoyable day. I was therefore absolutely bowled over when he insisted on giving me wages, consisting of the grand sum of half-a-crown, also known as two(shillings)-and-six(pence), an eighth of a pound and then the largest coin in circulation, and worth at least six pounds of today's money: probably more.

Last but not least there was Eric Rance, who ran a poultry farm on the hill above us. Eric was in his mid-thirties, a small fair-haired man who was both an idealist and something of a perfectionist. I was impressed by his farm, which was clearly his life. He had set it up himself, and everything had been done well. The hen runs, for example, had been constructed with six foot galvanised chicken wire in exactly straight lines; and the chicken houses, which were properly creosoted, had been put up with the aid of a spirit-level so that they were all dead-level. He had incubators operated by paraffin lamps which hatched a hundred chicks at a time; feeder houses for the young chicks; and he seemed to have all the traditional breeds of chicken. There were motherly Rhode Island Reds, Speckled Grey North Holland Blues, White Wyandots, and the highly excitable Leghorns.

During our holidays it was my delight to help Eric with his work: filling the lamps, mixing the wet chicken mash for the morning feed or broadcasting the afternoon feed of grain, which was a mixture of wheat and maize, or sweet-corn as maize is usually called today. The amount of feed was very carefully monitored, because this apparently idyllic farm lived with the constant danger of the outgoings exceeding the income. When the hens were laying well in the spring, the price would drop to 1/-(one shilling) per dozen; and would only rise to 2/9d per dozen in the winter, when of course production was down. However the miller's bill remained the same, summer and winter: a massive forty pounds (at least two thousand pounds of today's money) for two tons of chicken meal.

Gradually I spent more and more of my holiday-time on the farm, and the reason is obvious. My father was dead, my stepfather was a man of no authority in the home (though I was grateful to him for teaching me to bat properly) and my uncles were mostly dominated by their women-folk. Yet here in Eric Rance I had found a very masculine father-figure whom I could admire and who was also prepared to be not just a real friend but a mentor. He kindly but firmly taught me the right way to do things and the right way to behave in a wide range of circumstances. Indeed, I have often thought that if there are any traits in me of which I can be proud, then most of them derive from him.

In the meantime, dark and often dangerous news continued to percolate in from the outside world. I should say that by the time I was eight years old, the shadow of the coming war was already beginning to fall across our lives. At the time it was difficult for any of us to understand how Hitler was capable of inspiring such mass-hysteria in the German people. Looking back, I suppose that many Germans must have seen him as the only alternative to communism following their defeat in the 1914-1918 war, and the subsequent destruction of their wealth by runaway inflation.

I was nine-and-three-quarters when in September 1938 Neville Chamberlain flew to Munich to negotiate with Herr Hitler, and then flew back, bringing with him a piece of paper which, he said, meant 'Peace in our time!' We wanted to believe him, and he was the hero of the hour. Churchill by contrast was somewhere in the wings, thoroughly unpopular because he prophesied the inevitability of war and advocated re-armament.

Curiously enough, it was at about that time that my uncle Walter first told me about

Uranium 235, heavy water and the prospect of splitting the atom. I didn't fully understand what he was talking about, but it made a strong impression upon me, one that would be much reinforced by subsequent events.

And then one day in September 1939, towards the end of the summer holidays, we came down to our Sussex cottage from blackberrying on the Downs, to be told by Mr. Chamberlain on the wireless that a state of war existed between us and Nazi Germany.

CHAPTER THREE

Within a few months of the outbreak of the Second World War, rationing had been introduced. It would last right through the 1940s, and the weekly quantities we were allowed of cheese, butter, sugar and meat were unbelievably small by today's standards. As for petrol: only those deemed to be 'essential users' were allowed any, and most cars would be 'laid up' for the duration of the war. We also became used to conscription for all men aged between eighteen and forty-five, to identity cards, total black out, air raid wardens and air raid shelters; while the new question on everyone's lips was: "Don't you know there's a war on?" There were also new sets of initials to be learned, from DORA (the Defence of the Realm Act), WLA (the Women's Land Army), ATS (the Auxiliary Territorial Service), WRNS (the Women's Royal Naval Service) and WAAF (the Women's Auxiliary Air Force) through to the LDV. This referred to the Local Defence Volunteers, which became the Home Guard and years later was immortalised by actors such as Arthur Lowe, John Le Mesurier and Clive Dunn in television's *Dad's Army*.

My stepfather was evacuated to King's Lynn with the staff and pupils of Hackney Down School; but much to my regret the rest of us were effectively marooned in Sussex. If only we had been allowed to return to London, I would then have been evacuated to the countryside with my fellow-pupils at St. Aubyns, and the whole future course of my life would have been quite different. As it was, I was sent to Worthing High School, which occupied a large wooden building apparently put up on a 'temporary' basis after the last war.

We were joined by evacuees from Battersea Grammar School; though once the Germans had over-run France in June 1940 (a month after our own disastrous retreat over the beaches of Dunkirk), Worthing was within easy reach of German aeroplanes and no safer than London. Fortunately in the autumn of 1940 the RAF won what became known as the Battle of Britain, which preserved us from immediate invasion and almost certain defeat. From our air raid shelter in the garden I watched German and English aeroplanes engaged in 'dog-fights' overhead. Afterwards I would pick up dozens of spent brass bullet cases.

Unluckily I then went down with appendicitis and ended up in hospital. The surgeon visited me just before the operation, and asked how long an incision I wanted. I thought it would sound ungracious to tell him that I didn't want one at all, so I politely answered: "Would about two-and-a-half inches be all right?"

"And how many stitches shall I use when I sew you up again?"

"Would three be enough?"

It was a bizarre conversation; and much to my surprise, when I checked up afterwards with a ruler, the incision had been exactly two-and-a-half inches, and there were precisely three stitches. I remained uncertain whether this was pure chance, or whether I had changed medical practice.

At any rate, I was discharged much too soon, developed some sort of heart complication, and had to return to hospital for a second much longer spell. Curiously enough, during my convalescence I was invited to use their swimming-pool by some people in Storrington who had as their guest the 50-year-old Kenyan politician Jomo Kenyatta. I had many conversations with him. A refined and intelligent man, he told me without boasting that he was a prince in his own country, and that there was a mountain with the same name as his. He invited me to visit him in Kenya after the war, and I greatly regret that I was never able to take up his invitation, because after leading the Mau Mau terrorists who opposed British rule, he eventually (in 1963) led his country to independence.

By the time I was allowed home again, both Worthing High School and Battersea Grammar School had departed for safer regions, and so I had to start at yet another school. This was Steyning Grammar School, at the back of Brighton. It may have been a perfectly good school, but as a result of all the breaks and changes my education was in tatters; and from being proud of coming quite easily among the top three in my class at St. Aubyns, I was now ashamed to be struggling among the bottom three in my class at Steyning.

At home, in my stepfather's absence, I had to be the man of the house. It was I who pumped up our water, brought in the coal, chopped sticks, made our evening meal of soup and cleaned the household shoes. But our household was still a matriarchy. My efforts appeared to be totally unappreciated, and at the age of twelve I began to feel that I was a nobody, cared for by no-one.

One problem was that I had lost Eric Rance. Although neither a bully nor a racist, before the war he had been a member for many years of Sir Oswald Mosley's British Union of National Socialists. Eric was a great idealist and a patriot, and he genuinely believed that Mosley was the only man who could rescue us from the threat of communism. As a farmer, Eric was in a 'reserved occupation' which meant that he would not be conscripted into the army; but his political affinities meant that he was in great danger of being interned for the duration. At the same time, since he was allowed less and less concentrated feed for his poultry, he could no longer make his farm pay. In the circumstances he resolved to sell up and lose himself in the industrial Midlands, where he rightly believed he would have no difficulty in finding work.

In Eric's absence I found one diversion from the combined difficulties of home and school: that was keeping and breeding rabbits. I started by making a hutch, and I acquired a single doe. At the age of twelve I still knew nothing about the sex lives of either humans or animals, but Mr. Noyce came to my rescue. "Shall I bring my buck up to see your doe?" he enquired.

"I suppose it'll be company for her", I replied. And before very long I had a family of young rabbits. It was from them that I earned my first real income: eight rabbits at half-a-crown each, which came to a whole pound. I was learning!

In the autumn of 1941 I was shaken by the news that another school (my fifth) had been found for me. I was told that it was called Ardingly, that it was a boarding school, and that it would 'knock me into shape'. I felt that I was being punished, and things were made worse by my arriving at Ardingly several days after term had started. In the harsh environment of a minor public school of the 1940s, this was a bad tactical mistake. Even boys who had started only five days earlier had the edge on me.

When I arrived at this freezing cold penal colony at the back of beyond I was told that only one visiting-day per term was allowed, and none at all in the first term.

Added to that, juniors like me were not allowed to set foot beyond the school gates. I soon found that dining arrangements were primitive, and the food extremely basic. I had been allowed to bring with me a 'tuck-box' containing one fruit cake, one pound of jam and one pot of marmite. That would be my sole source of such luxuries for the rest of the thirteen-week term. Worst of all were the lavatories. They had no doors or seats, so I had to deal with the most private matters in full public view, while being subject to a barrage of obscenities and abuse.

Fagging was still the order of the day, and we new boys had to 'fag' for our prefects, which meant cleaning their shoes and their studies, making toast for them, and generally fetching and carrying. This was in addition to learning the unique school language and customs as best we could. Within the school hierarchy we were the lowest form of life; and I was still lower because games were considered to be very important; and on doctor's orders (I suppose as a precaution after reading my medical notes) I was 'off-games' for the whole of my first term. The only good news was that the Japanese attack on Pearl Harbour had brought the Americans into the war on our side, so at least we now stood a chance.

After the Christmas holidays Mother had to cajole and threaten me to force me back to school. It was a very cold winter and far, far worse then anything I had experienced the previous term. I resolved privately that I would not stay at Ardingly for another four years. In fact I would not go through another winter there. However, running away from school seemed like a bad idea, because the chances were that I would be recaptured and made to suffer. I have never enjoyed suffering, so I decided that I would run away from home as soon as possible after the start of the summer holidays of 1942. I neither deviated from nor regretted that decision.

In preparation, I hoarded my pocket-money (such as it was), and sold anything I had that was saleable. When I went home for the Easter holidays, I gathered together everything I had of any value, and thoroughly overhauled and oiled my bicycle in preparation for the longest bicycle ride I had ever attempted.

I went back to Ardingly for the summer term with something like a spring in my step. On the matter of leaving home, the die was cast and an unknown and exciting future beckoned. In the meantime, summer terms were always the best and I was determined to enjoy myself as much as possible. Not only would the weather be better, but also the school game in the summer was cricket, and as I mentioned I had been taught to bat by my step-father. He had kindly arranged for me to join one of his school teams, and one of my greatest pleasures had been going with him on Saturday afternoons to enjoy a good game of cricket on the school playing-fields out at Edmonton.

My cricketing heroes were Herbert Sutcliffe, Denis Compton and Don Bradman. And I felt there was always the possibility that with the combination of a good eye, a quick brain and a straight bat I could confound the most terrifying bowling. Though of tender years I might be asked to help out by a struggling first eleven, win the match for them by scoring a decisive century (not out), be asked to play for Sussex, be recognised by the test selectors as a child prodigy, become a national hero, and finally spend the rest of my life in sunny climes scoring multiple centuries interspersed with hat-tricks. In practice I never got further than the novices' eleven, and I believe my highest-ever score was fourteen — but it was a happy dream.

Another possible future of which I dreamed was becoming a stand-up comic, because I much admired Arthur Askey, Will Hay, George Formby and Jack Hulbert. Unfortunately I can't remember jokes, and my comic timing is abysmal. I think that above all I would have liked to become a composer or a concert pianist. To have created just one Moonlight Sonata would have been enough. And curiously, although my sense of pitch is a good deal less than perfect, when I'm alone I almost always have a melody running through my head. I have tunes for every possible mood, and scraps of song for every possible occasion. Sometimes the melodies bubble up from nowhere, tantalising me with their beauty; but sadly they remain locked in my head.

At last the end of the summer term arrived. My plans had been laid. In all of them, I had imposed upon myself a strict code of behaviour. I took no money from anyone; and although I raided the family's emergency store of food, which was hidden away in the roof of the garage, I took only what I could reasonably regard as my fair share.

So one morning early in August 1942, telling Mother that I was going for a cycle ride, I left home with all my worldly goods, including my coin collection, a small supply of cash, a map, a compass and my emergency rations. "Goodbye!" I called as I rode away.

"Goodbye!" she called after me.

It would be thirteen years before we saw each other again.

CHAPTER FOUR

It was a glorious summer's day, my bicycle was humming along, and I had a clear idea of where I was going. My aim was to find Eric Rance — I had his address in Birmingham — and to ask him for help. I had not forewarned him of my plans, because he would certainly have cautioned me and tried to deter me; but I was quite sure that once I had arrived on his door-step he would never give me away.

Trying to keep as low a profile as possible, I avoided central London, travelling instead in northerly loop which was probably more circuitous than I had intended, because as it was wartime all the sign-posts had been removed. I stopped very rarely for refreshment, and was in fact still cycling when dusk began falling. I then pulled off the road I was on, opened a gate on the right-hand-side of the road and let myself into a field where I ate my supper, put on my coat and fell fast asleep. When I awoke I was so cold that I decided to start cycling at once in order to get warm again; and I had only cycled fifty yards when I realised with a shock that I had spent the night almost next-door to the main entrance of an army camp.

Fortunately no-one had spotted me. The day warmed up, and I was soon in Henley-on-Arden, making good speed towards Birmingham, and only about fifteen miles from my destination. Coming in the other direction a massive convoy of army lorries filled with civilians passed me by. They looked utterly dispirited, and I learned later that there had been an air-raid on Birmingham during the night, and all these people had been bombed out and were being evacuated.

It was still morning when I found Eric's flat on the outskirts of Birmingham. I was delighted to see him. He was less enthusiastic: not surprisingly, as I was likely to bring him nothing but trouble. But, as I had anticipated, he would not compel me to return to my family.

My first action was to write a letter to my mother. I was afraid she would think I had met with an accident, and I did not want to worry her more than was necessary. So I said simply that I had left home, that I did not intend to return and that I would make my own way in the world. Eric arranged for this letter to be posted in London so that no tell-tale postmark could give her a clue as to my real whereabouts.

Eric and I had also agreed straight away that I could not live hidden away like a fugitive. This meant that I needed a new identity and a convincing cover story.

Eric himself had already changed his name, by obtaining and then doctoring the identity card of a Mr. Yeomanson. Deleting the Yeo had made him into Andrew James Manson, the name we later used for the company we founded. A similar card was procured for me from the same source. Retaining only the 'man' of 'Yeomanson', and adding 'Free' in front, I became R. J. Freeman. That initial 'R' was the only part of my original name; but now it stood for Robert and I was usually called Bob Freeman, the name by which I have been known ever since.

Among his new friends, Eric was now known as Jim; and he and I became honorary cousins. My next task was to find work.

Fortunately there was a labour shortage. Jim was already established as a civilian mechanic in some Army Auxiliary workshops (formerly the 'Tricroft Motor Combine'), and I secured a job at the same place as an apprentice auto-electrician. Applying for the job was alarming. I was interviewed by the overseer of the works Mr. Robinson, who appeared to be at one and the same time the civilian director of Tricroft and the Army Commanding Officer. I then had to go for a medical examination and to register at the Ministry of Labour, and I couldn't help feeling that someone would discover who I was and that I had run away from home. However, it all went without a hitch.

We electricians were primarily responsible for reconditioning the electrics of the convoys of Bedford and Morris commercial army lorries of all sizes which passed through the workshops. I started work with Arthur Evans. He had been a turner, which required a great deal of strength, but had lost his right arm in a motor-cycling accident and had retrained as an electrician. For someone like me with both arms, he was an inspiring example of what could be done with only one arm and a great deal of application. I enjoyed my work, which kept stretching me. Although I was often very dirty and sometimes very tired I was never disillusioned: except perhaps at the end of my very first week when, after deductions, I received only 19/7d instead of the £1/2s/6d upon which I had been counting.

We electricians were also responsible for all the electrical services in the entire workshops, so whenever tools or lights failed, the cry went up: "Electrician!" I was terrified by this part of my new duties. The point was that the workshops were simply a series of bricked-in railway arches, with dampness pouring out of the walls, and sometimes even running water streaming down them and around the iron-clad fuse boxes. The ancient fuses in those boxes clung like limpets in their sockets; but I did not dare to touch the damp wall with my free hand in case I received an electric shock which might throw me off the ladder on which I was perched.

Incidentally, there were no fluorescent light tubes: instead there were light-bulbs, seized in large screw fittings inside stove enamel shades, and attached to especially strong 'catinary' wires which were strung out across each archway and supported the electric cable.

Soon after my arrival we had a new foreman in the imposing figure of Mr. Hall, who was over six foot three inches tall and proportionately broad. Unfortunately he was also totally bald, a fact which he tried but failed to disguise with a very crude wig, surmounted by an atrocious peaked cap. In those days workmen wore ordinary overalls, but foremen wore special pale-brown overalls known as 'cow-gowns'. And when Mr. Hall emerged from his tiny office, dipping his head to get through the door and wearing an extra-capacious cow-gown, he looked as he moved slowly on his large flat feet like a square-rigged galleon under full sail.

We were told that we should respect Mr. Hall. But a man has to earn respect; and of this he was incapable. The result was that wicked little beret-wearing Jack Slater began a conspiracy to ridicule Mr. Hall, a conspiracy which also served as an effective advanced warning of the new foreman's arrival. As Mr. Hall progressed through the works, people would chant in muffled tones "our congenial foreman to whom we raise our hats", while at the same time going through the motions of raising their hats, real or (in most cases) imaginary. Mr. Hall's normally sallow face coloured up and his monstrously-large frame shook with ill-concealed rage, but there was little he could do about this mass opposition.

However, Mr. Hall had a number of aces up his sleeve. For example, he was the only source of official requisitions upon the stores, a necessity if one was to have any hope of success with the storeman Mr. Shenston. Although it was wartime and we were engaged in 'high priority' work, hours were wasted at the stores hatch trying to wheedle something from Mr. Shenston. Even with the right piece of paper signed by Mr. Hall, it was not always possible to get what was needed. When clothes rationing was at its peak, the hardest commodity to obtain from the stores was a piece of clean cotton rag. This was an essential for intricate work, and mechanics prized it almost as highly as their tools.

Any particularly large job was often undertaken by Jack Slater and Charlie Hollins together. Charlie, an ex-farmer, must have been twice Jack's weight. Wearing his huge boiler suit, and with that and his great bear-like paws covered with black oil, he looked capable of dealing single-handed with anything up to a tank; but his enormous size concealed a lovely mellow character, and he was always willing to give advice.

Our machinist was Len Crump, who was lean, slim-faced and (at only thirty-something) nearly bald. If anything could be made, milled, drilled, cut or turned on his ancient machines, he was the man for the job. He was also a man of great good humour; and while he worked a constant stream of extremely naughty stories flowed from his lips. I didn't understand all of them; but if I was ever feeling at all depressed, Len could always cheer me up.

The system was fuelled by a monthly bonus scheme which helped us to achieve a 400% increase in production. But the bonus was only paid on vehicles which had passed the final test inspection, and this was a source of considerable friction between the production men and the test department. On the last day of each month vehicles would be sent back by Albert and Bernard with chalk marks indicating loose screws and cleats, and they and the mechanics would be at it hammer and tongs, with the mechanics arguing that the production department was nit-picking. However, it was only when Albert had given his final approval that the vehicle could be sent for its new coat of camouflage, and go back to war.

That was satisfying. We knew we were doing important work, and with luck our efforts would not be in vain. In October 1942 Montgomery had turned the tide of battle in North Africa with his victory at El Alamein and had become a national hero, while the Russians were draining Hitler's resources on the Eastern Front.

In general there was a great deal of good-will in the works, and personally I found a degree of camaraderie which I had never before experienced. However a few people called me 'Oxford Boy' because they couldn't quite accept my accent; and on one occasion my previous identity was almost discovered. Unknown to me, there had been a notice in *The News of the World* offering a massive £200 reward for news of my whereabouts. One of the lads, George Price, discussed with Jim the fact that he thought I matched the description. "I managed to laugh it off", Jim told me afterwards, "but it was too close for comfort!"

The fact that Jim and I shared a southern accent was noted elsewhere. Instead of making breakfast at home, we always set out early and then stopped for a cup of tea and a sandwich at Garibaldi's Cafe before starting work. Nat, as the tubby Italian owner Nathaniel Garibaldi was affectionately known, always thought of us as gentlemen, and would cheerfully sing out: "Two t's for two g's!"

We worked a 52-and-a-half hour working week, which ran from 8 am to 6 pm from Monday to Friday (with an unpaid half-hour break for lunch at one o'clock) and from 8 am to 1 pm on Saturdays. This was standard at the time, and I well remember that during one tea-break there was a discussion about whether a five-day week might become the norm when the war was over. I said little, but thought this was so unlikely as to be quite ludicrous. In passing I must say that I have been proved wrong so often that whatever success I later achieved must have depended more upon luck and the ability to survive my mistakes than upon any great foresight on my part.

Future business success occupied my thoughts a great deal. Very soon after I had teamed up with Jim, we had opened an account at the nearest bank, which happened to be a branch of Lloyds in Deritend. Little did we realise that this would be the start of a business association lasting more than thirty years. Our arrangement was that whatever our joint earnings (and Jim's increased when he accepted the job of running the reorganised 'Inward Testing Department'), we would bank £4 and live on the rest. This wasn't always easy, but we were determined to create a 'grub stake', in other words a sum of money large enough for us to start a business of our own.

On Saturday afternoons we combed the Stratford and Ladypool Roads looking for bargains which could make us money. So many things were in short supply and only available (even with the necessary permits) in wartime 'utility' form, that there was a firm demand for good second-hand equipment, such as wireless sets that actually worked. I found that I could buy a broken two-valve wireless for 7/6d (worth around £19 today), fix it up over the weekend, including polishing the case, and then sell it at work for £2/10s/0d (worth around £120 today) — a healthy profit.

In my spare time I had bought *Teach Yourself Electricity,* passed the exam which in those days was included at the end of the book, and won a further volume. This time I chose *Teach Yourself Radio,* which I had soon digested. I had unbounded confidence in myself: a valuable asset, even if it stemmed from not realising how little I knew!

We soon decided that our 'grub stake' would never grow fast enough if we continued to live in comparative luxury in a two-guinea (£2/2s/0d) per week fully furnished flat. So we moved to No. 105 Garrison Lane, where we had found an empty shop with living accommodation above. This cost us only £1 per week, and we were able to use the shop premises as our workshop.

The only risk we ran here (since we were both effectively 'on the run') was from the nosiness of the diminutive 5-foot-nothing newsagent Mr. Partridge, whose shop was next door at No. 107. We bought our daily paper from him, and that was no problem because he was always busy in the shop when we called in. Unfortunately we had an outside toilet in the back yard; and Mr. Partridge was so keen to find out all about us that he kept a large box in his own back yard, so that whenever the opportunity arose he could jump up on it and talk to us over the garden wall. It must have been frustrating for him when we answered his lengthy enquiries with such brief and unenlightening replies.

We sometimes earned extra money on Sundays after hearing that one of our Directors Mr. Goodway wanted volunteers to work in his garden. Goodway appeared to be the money man behind Tricroft, and supported not only a Rolls but also a 1937 American

Cord, made by the Auburn Automobile Company with an electrically-controlled gearbox. Unfortunately we were paid through the firm after a very high rate of tax had been deducted; but although our gardening therefore earned us less than £2 per week between us, it was all grist to the mill.

My wages were further increased when I successfully applied for a job as an assistant in Jim's department. I began by testing vehicles when they arrived, and making out job-sheets of what work needed to be done to them in the workshops. But as the number of vehicles increased, the works yard was no longer large enough, so we acquired a vehicle park at Marston Green, Elmdon, where Birmingham Airport is today. Very soon Mr. Robinson had instructed Jim to teach me to drive, initially so that I could ferry vehicles to and from this park. There were still no driving tests; so towards the end of 1943, at the age of 15 (I was thought to be 17, having added two years to my age when joining the firm), I found myself driving heavy army lorries all over Birmingham and beyond. [And when I later progressed to driving private cars, I thought them very light and difficult to manage.]

Being able to get out on the road was a tremendous advantage in one important respect. Neither Jim nor I had any ration books (not having dared to apply for them in our new 'false' identities), so it had always been difficult getting enough to eat; but now that I was driving lorries I could stop at transport cafes, where it was always possible to get bacon sandwiches, egg and chips and so on.

It was at about this time that I noticed a classified advertisement in the *Birmingham Post* which read:

Three-and-a-half acres of land, well watered by running brook,
Shropshire/Montgomeryshire border, £150, Clarke & Son Solicitors, Swan Hill, Shrewsbury.

I discussed the matter with Jim, and we decided to buy it. Why? Because neither of us liked living in a city, and it was exciting to think of owning a little stretch of countryside. We did not have the full £150, but we sent off a 10% deposit of £15 which was enough to secure the property, and then we had to set about finding the balance.

So began a frenzy of working overtime, of buying and putting in order and selling; and of selling treasured possessions: even my coin collection went, and so did our bicycles. At length we raised the money and became joint-owners of a parcel of land on the Welsh Border.

Our new purpose in life was to go and take possession of our first piece of freehold real estate. There was no petrol for private motoring so our only option, having sold our bicycles, was to build two new ones. We went to the local scrap-yard and acquired two cycle frames, four wheels and sundry other parts. The only parts we bought new were pedal rubbers, handle grips, brake blocks, lights and a pot of paint.

Even then, it was not until the early summer of 1944 that we qualified for a week's holiday and set off on our bicycles. We chose to take the scenic route, setting out on the Hagley road and then cycling via Halesowen, Kidderminster, Bewdley, Cleobury Mortimer, Ludlow and Craven Arms. At one point a wrong turn added ten miles to our journey.

Finally, finding ourselves on the right road about half-way between Bishops Castle and Minsterley, we stopped and asked a man whether he could direct us to the Pant Field, Runnis near Hyssington. "You've come to the right place", said the man slowly. He went on to tell us that his name was Tom Watkin, and that he and his missus lived at Runnis Cottage. "Look down there", he added, pointing to the land immediately beside us. "That's Pant Field."

It was like reaching the Promised Land. We were dog-tired and the light was waning. We went onto our land, found somewhere safe for our bicycles, and had something to eat. Then, having found two convenient trees, we stretched a piece of rope between them and hung a piece of canvas over it to make a ridge tent. Finally, we walked right round our three-and-a-half acres, savouring every step, enjoying each bird and tree and blade of grass, and taking especial pleasure from our bubbling brook. The West Onny at this point was in fact more than just a bubbling brook: it formed the boundary between England and Wales. Then we returned to our tent well-satisfied, wrapped ourselves in groundsheets and blankets and slept sound and content.

It was cold the next morning, and we were stiff from cycling. So we brewed tea and walked around our acres again, to warm us before the sun came up. For the next two days we maintained our camp and explored the neighbourhood. We were extremely pleased with our purchase: it was a base of our own, a place to which we could retreat from the warring world. However, the country was still in the throes of 'fifth column fever', and anyone whose presence couldn't be accounted for, was suspected of being a spy. We were also repeatedly being told that 'Walls have ears!' So we decided not to stay on our newly-acquired land for too long; and we cycled back to Birmingham by a different and more direct route, through Shrewsbury, Wellington, Shifnal and Wolverhampton.

Memory sometimes plays us cruel tricks; and of Shrewsbury, which was destined to play such a large part in my future, I can remember absolutely nothing. We must have passed through the town centre because the then by-pass was closed during the war, when it was used as an army vehicle park.

All went well until we were cycling past Cosford Aerodrome. This was subject to high-level security, and there were notices saying 'No stopping under any circumstances!' This was the moment when my bicycle, with its much-repaired inner tubes, managed to have two punctures. We had no option but to stop and repair them, while expecting at any moment to be arrested as suspected spies by the Air Force police. Our guardian angel must have been watching over us that day, because no-one questioned us, and we cycled back into Birmingham tired but free, and in the best of spirits.

Our spirits were further improved not long after our return by the war news. We had already invaded Italy (then described as 'the soft underbelly of Europe'), and now on 6 June 1944 came D-Day, with Allied Forces landing on the Normandy beaches. Soon we had consolidated our position (with supplies being landed via the pre-fabricated 'Mulberry Harbour', whose story was an epic in itself), and had begun the liberation of France.

Meanwhile, having sold our bicycles on our return from Wales, Jim and I had bought our first car, a 1934 Wolseley Hornet which cost us £15. We stripped it out mechanically and took the engine to our home workshop to be overhauled. After several months of evening work, it had been rebuilt. When we gave it a road-test, we found that it went beautifully. We parked it proudly in the works yard; and when Jack Slater saw it, he asked: "How much do you want for it?"

"We're not interested in selling."

"Everything has its price!" he replied. "How much would you take?"

Jim and I had a private conference. We genuinely had not thought of selling. In the end, we thought of the highest possible price, and came back to Jack.

"I'm sorry, Jack, but we wouldn't dream of taking less than £60."

"I'll take it!" he said at once.

Within a few weeks we had purchased a 1938 Opel Olympia, very unpopular at that time because it was German. After minor adjustments and one journey, this too was snapped up. Once again, we had bought for £15 and sold for £60!

By the beginning of August we had used our spare time to recondition a further three vehicles, making a profit out of each. The result was that (apart from our three-and-a-half acres) we had approximately £285 of capital between us. The commercial bit was between our teeth. Nor were we needed any more for the war effort. Germany had unconditionally surrendered back on 7 May; and very soon the use of atomic bombs on Hiroshima (8 August) and Nagasaki (9 August) would lead to the surrender of Japan. We were ready to strike out on our own, and we handed in our notice.

It was in August 1945, in a canal-side yard rented from Albert for 30/-(thirty shillings) a week, that we founded 'A.J. Manson: Motor Engineers and Sales Agents'. During our first week's trading, we purchased a 1935 Ford 10 for £95, and sold it for £110. After expenses of £1/10s/0d, we had made a net profit of £13/10s/0d. So we had not only covered our overheads, but had also made more than our previous joint week's wages.

Using scrap timber and second-hand corrugated-iron sheeting, we roofed an area just large enough for us to work on one car at a time. So it would have been a major disaster to have been stuck with an unsaleable vehicle on our hands.

Our early success depended largely upon knowledge gained during our war-time work. We were able to test vehicles and to diagnose what was wrong with great accuracy. We also had great confidence in our ability to dismantle and repair any part of the vehicle, from the engine to the back axle. We had learned to apply ourselves rigorously to the work in hand. We had also learned not only how to find essential spare parts, but also how to make items if we found that they were totally unobtainable.

Jim in particular was a wonderful innovator. We would run up against a seemingly insoluble problem involving a missing part. Instead of panicking, we would settle down for a cup of tea; and then Jim would begin walking round the place, pick something up, and reckon that he could turn it into what was required. Watching him perform these apparent miracles gave me the confidence to do the same.

One example of our innovative approach was in the way we dealt with a Rover 12, whose coach-work body needed to be completely restored. The manufacturer could not help us, so we used wood from an ancient piano bought for only 5/-. We began to revel in challenges, and profited from working on a great many unusual foreign cars, such as a Czechoslovakian Tatra, a Canadian Auburn, and a Packard Eight which we managed to sell to our ex-boss.

As for recreation: we never smoked or drank alcohol, but when we had enough petrol we motored down to our three-and-a-half acre estate. People had begun to hear of us as car specialists from Birmingham, and we were soon being approached on the subject of reliable second-hand cars, which were hard to get. Our first deal was rapidly followed by two more, and we could see that (for once) business and pleasure could be profitably mixed.

However, we didn't want to go on camping on our land for ever; and by the summer of 1946 we had made enough money to buy a wooden four-room bungalow for £100. It had to be dismantled from its site near the canal in Birmingham and transported by lorry something which Albert arranged for £15. When it was delivered in its dismantled state, it looked like a pile of wooden rubbish. However it had soon been resurrected into its former state, with two bedrooms, a kitchen-diner, and a living-room with a large log stove. Although this began as our second base, events rapidly overtook us. We found ourselves doing so well on the Welsh borders that within a few months we had given notice both on our Garrison Lane home and our Birmingham canal-side yard.

We had a few glorious months and then on 15 January 1947 we were hit by the notoriously bad winter of 1947. The dreadful weather did not lift until the end of March, and until then we had no income. The main road would be blocked for up to five days at a time, the side roads for weeks. There were no snow-ploughs in those days, and the snow-drifts would be slowly cleared by German and Italian prisoners-of-war. On many occasions we had to walk the five-and-a-half miles to Bishops Castle and the five-and-a-half miles back again, in the most appalling conditions, simply to buy food. Not only were we unable to travel around buying and selling, but we had built no garage in which to renovate our vehicles when the weather was too bad to work outside.

The 1947 summer was as good as the winter had been bad; but we were determined not to be caught out by another bad winter, so a garage had to be built. We decided that this should be 12 foot wide by 16 foot long, which would give us room to work on one car, or to store two. A concrete floor was unthinkable because of the cost, but we dug it out and filled it with stone chippings. We then made a frame with second-hand 6" x 3" timbers, which we cut long-ways to make 3" x 2" joists. We wanted a building that would last, so we lashed out on new galvanised iron, flat for the walls and corrugated for the roof. It was in this new building that we began producing our great works.

We scoured the area for cars needing restoration which could be bought cheaply. We then did everything that was needed not only mechanically, but also in terms of renewing bodywork, painting, cleaning and upholstering, to ensure that each car, however old, left us in the best possible condition. Sales were never a problem; and because our standards were high, one sale almost always led to another.

We were hard task-masters to ourselves; and we operated a strict but simple form of book-keeping. At the end of each month we calculated our total current net worth. Then we calculated the net profit that we had made during that month; and if the figures did not tally when we added the net profit to our total net worth for the previous month, then we held an inquest to account for the discrepancy. The object of this exercise was to ensure that we did not dissipate the fruits of our labours.

By mid-1947 we were ready to expand further and for £200 we bought the leasehold of the Talbot Garage in Much Wenlock. Charlie Hollins from the Army Auxiliary works joined us to run the business and we made a round-trip of 60 miles each day to get it off the ground. However we soon felt too tied down by the dreary routine of managing a conventional business, and we sold out to Charlie for a modest profit. I am glad to say that over the years he built up a very successful business, not only locally but also in exporting ex-government commercial vehicles; and he was able to build his own home, get married, and eventually take early retirement.

By the end of 1948 (when I had reached the grand old age of twenty), we had instructed an architect to produce drawings for a new brick bungalow to replace our wooden one. It was fortunate that part of our land was in Wales, or we would never have secured a building permit. As it was, while the bungalow was being built, a very small car drew up, and from it a massive 18-stone 6 foot-6 inches monster unwound himself. Drawing himself up to his full height, he looked at us fiercely before barking out: "Who's in charge here?" When no-one seemed very keen to take responsibility, he added, still more fiercely, "Under whose authority is this building going on?"

My reply, "The Montgomeryshire County Council", seemed to make him shrink visibly. He was from Shropshire County Council, and had come out of his area without realising it. Not only did he cause us no more trouble, but (once we had cheered him up with a cup of tea) we convinced him that his Morris 8 was unsuitable for a man of his size and rank, and we sold him a Wolsley 10 which we had restored.

Runnis Garage

By July 1949 we were able to move into our new home, having sold the wooden bungalow for only £10 less than we had paid for it. In the meantime we had recouped a substantial part of the £1,400 cost of the bungalow by selling re-conditioned cars and vans to the builder and his employees.

Most of our business came from personal contacts like these. In particular, we gradually acquired the trust of the local farmers. We would drive a reconditioned car to them for a demonstration, and what happened would follow a predictable pattern. After talking to them in the farm-yard we would go out for a trial run; then we would drive a bargain; and then we would very often be offered lunch or supper, and sometimes a most welcome side-deal of eggs or ham.

If we had not been invited to dine by the farmer, we usually feasted at a tea shop or transport cafe on the way home. This was a necessary extravagance if we were to keep ourselves fit for work.

The next stage in the development of our business was the purchase in the autumn of 1949 of a large Nissen Hut, 60 foot long, 35 foot wide and 15 foot high. Including delivery all the way from Bures in Suffolk, this cost us £180. Once again our guardian angel must have been looking after us, because we had erected three spans of the frame-work when a gust of wind caused the whole thing to collapse around us. We could easily have been killed. As it was, we just had to set to and dismantle the whole thing and start all over again.

We had spared no expense, making a floor of 3' by 2' paving slabs laid on a bed of ashes, and adding an imposing frontage to the original Nissen building. Starting with just one local lad, Graham Gittins, we soon had five men reconditioning cars in this new building, which we thought of as a model workshop. During the week we bought stock and supervised the work; and at week-ends we sold. We found that taking out classified advertisements in the *Wellington Journal and Shrewsbury News* brought us between 40 and 50 potential customers, starting on Friday evening and not stopping till late on Sunday.

By June 1950 we felt so confident that we decided we could take our first proper holiday: one which was much needed, and well deserved. Setting out in a 1947 M.G. model TC two-seater, we headed for Scotland. Paying between 12/6d and 15/- for bed and breakfasts, we stayed the first night at Aviemore — long before it became a famous resort — and motored on via Blairgowrie and Inverness right up to John O'Groats. Then we turned west, and drove through Lochinvar and Ullapool to Oban. At Oban there is the most magical view from the harbour looking out towards the islands, and we could not resist taking the McBraynes steamer all the way to Stornoway in the Outer Hebrides. Calvinism was still strong on the islands, and on our return from Stornoway we loaded at one minute past midnight, so as to avoid sailing on the Sabbath.

We returned to work like giants refreshed.

Business was not always straightforward, being dominated for some years by the amount of the basic petrol ration, which had a strong effect upon both the demand for cars, and the prices at which they could be sold. When petrol rationing ended, we increased our potential market by providing hire-purchase facilities, and increased our profits by making a substantial commission on both hire-purchase agreements and car insurance. However the market swung down again when the Government imposed strict controls on hire-purchase, increasing the necessary deposit from 25% to 50%, and cutting the repayment period from 24 months to 12.

Every year we went to the motor-show at Earl's Court in London, and in those days the motor-show was always combined with a boat-show. The result was that in October 1951, though neither of us had ever done any sailing, Jim and I were up at the motor-show when we decided to buy a new 21-foot Fisherman cruiser which came complete with new 10-30 h.p. Watermota Ford engine, sail rig and open cockpit for under £600. I don't know whether in my case our sudden purchase had anything to do either with my having enjoyed Arthur Ransome's *Swallows and Amazons* when I was a boy, or with the happy hours I had once spent at Connaught Water.

The following May we went down to Dover, took delivery of her from Southern Yacht Services, and named her *Venturer*. For our first voyage we hired Captain Gare, an old sea captain who sailed with us first to Newhaven and then on to Cowes. Even the business of coming into harbour was fascinating for us beginners: there are so many things to be borne in mind, particularly the rise and fall of the tide. On the third morning, having watched the skipper set the course for two days and had the basic principles of navigation explained to me, also having spent a considerable time studying the points of the compass, I worked out the course for Weymouth. Except for one small mistake, which might have landed us in the middle of Swanage, I did quite well. From Weymouth we sailed on to Teignmouth, Brixham, Falmouth, St. Ives, Milford Haven, Cardigan, and what was to be our 'home' port of Aberdovey.

'The last part of this final hop, from Aberystwyth to Aberdovey', as I wrote

Venturer

in an article which was accepted and published by *Motor Boat and Yachting* in October 1952, 'proved the worst of the trip. A strong N.W. wind blew up and things were far from comfortable. We did not know it at the time, but two Army officers in an 18-ft. sailing boat coming from Ireland to Aberdovey that same day were unfortunately lost. We made it all right, slipped through the harbour bar with very little to spare and into calm water and our destination at exactly 15.00 hours on Sunday, May 25 1952.

But the excitement was not over yet; we had only been ashore a couple of hours and had a meal when some people came running up the beach shouting "They've turned over!" We quickly untied and went to the help of a girl and two men who were clinging to their overturned craft. We managed to get a line fixed to the boat and towed it in and beached it. They thanked us and said they hoped we should never be in a position to need the compliment returned.

For my article, by the way, I was paid the grand sum of seven guineas; and this encouraged me to write a set of children's stories which was published as the *Read Me A Story Book*.

However we were unhappy with *Venturer*. Probably no boat is perfect, being (for example) either too long or too short, having too much draft or too little; but Venturer had a non-self-draining cockpit, and so (especially after that alarming last leg) we thought her insufficiently sea-worthy for the long voyages we had in mind. We therefore sold her, and sent her south (by road this time) to the Isle of Wight. As for finding a new boat: we put our names down on the tender list of the RNLI (Royal Naval Lifeboat Institution) for redundant life-boats, which we presumed should be suitably sea-worthy.

Business continued to be reasonably good; but we assumed that the demand for used vehicles would fade as soon as new cars were readily available. At that time, anyone able to get delivery of any new car, whether it be a Ford, an Austin Morris or a Vauxhall, would have to pay between £300 and £400 including taxes but then, having run it for a few thousand miles, could sell it at double its cost. This state of affairs could not last indefinitely, and we decided that the best way of establishing a more permanent business was to open a petrol station.

First we applied for planning consent for a new petrol station on our own road frontage; and then in 1952, when that application was turned down, we purchased a site with a blacksmith's shop and one petrol pump four miles down the road in Hope. We redeveloped this site with a new building and petrol pumps, and opened it for business in June 1953, with flags and bunting to celebrate the coronation of Queen Elizabeth II.

We named our new business the 'Quick Service Station', because we believed that was what forecourt customers most wanted; and they certainly ribbed our staff if they didn't get it!

At that time the Regent Oil Company (later Texaco) had taken over the original ROP (Russian Oil Products) depots, and were keen to build up a chain of outlets. We wrongly assumed that if we developed our business and bought their products, they would back us with marketing support and volume discounts. Despite our disappointment we carried on, buying a site in Crewe and an existing but run-down road-side garage at Little Compton near Moreton-in-the-Marsh. Both these were redeveloped. The site in Crewe became another 'Quick Service Station', and its resident manager was Mick Johnson, who was small in stature but great-hearted, and worked with us on and off until 1982. The Little Compton garage became the 'Oil Well', and its manager was Glyn Price with whom we would also have a long-standing business association.

In 1954, having made the Fishguard to Rosslare crossing with a 2.4 litre Jaguar, we toured right round Ireland. First we headed west, and drove through Waterford, on to Cork, and out into the remote west. In those days it was even wilder and more beautiful than it is today. We then motored north through Killarney, with its famous lakes and its horse-drawn 'jaunting cars', and on to Connemara and Donegal. Leaving the Republic behind, we crossed into a Northern Ireland still fifteen years away from the Troubles, and drove on to Portrush and the Giants' Causeway. Then we turned south for Belfast, Dublin and home.

It had been a wonderful holiday, and on our return I said to Jim: "You remember that property for sale we noticed in the west of County Cork? I wish I'd made a note of the Estate Agent's name and address!"

Jim agreed with me; and the result was that before many months had passed we were back in the Republic once again, savouring the charms of Bantry Bay and Glengarriff while we looked at a number of properties. Eventually we settled on a sound little house with stone and mud walls two feet thick. It overlooked the sea, and was known locally as 'Kate O'Leary's cottage'.

The story was that Kate had been brought up by her aunt and uncle; and when they died she was left in the cottage on her own. It was a primitive place with no bath, toilet or kitchen, though there was a water tap in the road outside; and Kate O'Leary had done her cooking in a huge pot, hung from a bracket over a roaring fire, in a fire-place large enough to stand in. She boiled water for her tea, to which she was devoted, over the same fire. Then one day she and her tea-pot had simply disappeared.

Our estate agent, Mr. O'Leary (no relation) liked telling us the story of what had probably happened next. "De T'eory", he would begin, "which has niver be-un en despute" was that Kate, making tea late at night, had taken her tea-pot down the garden, as she usually did, to throw the tea-leaves into the sea far below. On this occasion, however, she threw with so much force that the tea-pot went into the sea, with herself still holding on to it. Her body had never been recovered, and some wicked people had suggested that she might have gone off to the city with a man. But, as Mr O'Leary always concluded triumphantly, "How would dat account for de missin' tay-pot?"

We paid £750 for Kate O'Leary's cottage. At that time, the Irish imposed a tax of 50% on all property bought by foreigners. But when we voiced our concern Mr O'Leary told us: "Sure, 'tis no problem. We'll be charging you £50 for the cottage, on which you will have to pay de tax. De garden gate will be £700, and dere's no tax on dat." After which, we decided that we had no alternative but to change the name from 'O'Leary's cottage' to 'The Golden Gate'.

Over the next three years we travelled to Ireland twice a year to carry out a major programme of renovation. We did everything ourselves, putting in new windows, doors, plumbing and wiring. We worked long hours and thoroughly enjoyed every minute.

O'Leary's Cottage' is transformed into 'The Golden Gate'.

I began to feel that I had gained enough self-confidence and independence to be able to meet my mother and the rest of my family again without being dominated or submerged by them as I had been in the past. So towards the end of 1954, at the age of twenty-six, I contacted our London solicitor, John Yates and asked him how best to proceed. The result was that early in 1955 he and I met in Jury's Hotel in Dublin to discuss the matter.

It was our first meeting. He looked just like the actor Robert Morley and at sixteen stone was significantly overweight; but I found him most understanding and accommodating. Indeed, he became a life-long friend, combining business with pleasure on his twice-yearly visits to Shropshire. After a friendship of some twenty-eight years, he died very suddenly at the age of 65 in 1983, and I still miss him very much. What shall I say of him? The cocktail of his friendship contained so many ingredients that it is hard to know where to begin.

He was certainly a great gourmet, enjoying good food just as much whether it was served in the imposing dining-rooms of the Junior Carlton Club or the Mansion House, or in my own home or in one of his two bachelor pads. His enthusiasm for good food drew unexpected gastronomic delights equally from young gentlemen or aged lady retainers, and certainly helped to inspire my own wife's delicious Pavlovas and Salmon Mousses. He liked good wine, and also had a fondness for pink gin: I well remember his initiating me into the mystery of Angostura Bitters.

As for his undoubted wisdom and extensive legal knowledge: they were matched only by his knowledge of fruit and flowers, an interest which he actively pursued as a life-member of both the Chelsea and the Shrewsbury Horticultural Societies. When I was married he was a frequent visitor; and if he spotted a gap somewhere in my garden, he would say nothing but at the appropriate time of the year for planting, a suitable bush or tree would arrive, with a note about where it should be placed. He also became one of my son Philip's Godfathers, a duty which he performed with great acumen.

I often thought that the range of his interests and the breadth of his character were in some way reflected by the striking contrast between the cars he owned. For shopping he kept an ancient Triumph Herald from which he had some difficulty in extricating himself. For travelling, on the other hand, he used a massive Mercedes Convertible. Invariably he drove with the roof open, wearing an ancient leather coat and a flying helmet. This drew almost as much attention to him as his unconventional driving; while the open format caused havoc to the hairdos of his women passengers.

His houses were similarly diverse. His minute terraced house in Kensington was crammed with memorabilia from his foreign travels. These were undertaken either to visit clients in faraway places, or in his capacity as Chief Common Councillor. In this latter role he accompanied Lord Mayors of London to such delightful places as Australia, Thailand, British Columbia, Kenya, Hong Kong and Portugal. His souvenirs of these visits were supplemented by dozens of limited-edition Collector's Plates with floral designs, to which he was happily addicted. And in his back yard — it could hardly be described as a garden — he somehow managed to nurture a prized collection of 160 Camellias.

On the other hand there was his large country house at Tilford near Farnham. His hospitality was not only generous but legendary, and would stretch to accommodate my entire family overnight on our way to an early departure from Gatwick. Tilford was the centre of his gardening activities; and nothing pleased him more than to serve us with a meal in which all the various vegetables and fruit which appeared on the table had come from his own vegetable garden. New potatoes, sprouts, broccoli, lettuces, raspberries, strawberries, blueberries, he grew them all and all were equally prized. And if an occasional 'wriggly' was found lurking in the salad or the raspberries, no matter. That just proved that they were fresh from the garden.

It was on John Yates's advice that, after our first meeting back in 1955, I officially changed my name by deed poll from R.M. Day to R.M.J. Freeman. I then met him again at his London offices, to which my mother had also been summoned for our first meeting for some thirteen years.

Mother had aged, of course; but then she had always seemed old to me. Her determination was undimmed. Indeed, it was one of her greatest qualities, and perhaps I had inherited it from her. Meeting her on an adult basis, I began to think of this formidable lady as one of the last of the Victorians, full of practical energy. However, it was soon clear that Mother thought that she had got me back. She desperately wanted me to buy a house and start a business near her, where she could re-establish her influence over me. So far as I was concerned, that was out of the question. From then on we kept in touch, but usually at a distance. Indeed it would later become a family joke that Mother and I got on extremely well — provided we were separated by at least two hundred miles.

As for my stepfather: I could now see him as an outstandingly good man, but one can have too much of anything, and extreme virtue comes very close to being a vice, in that it can spoil your own life and other people's. The poor man had certainly suffered a great deal as a result of my departure, because Mother had tried to blame it all on him. I privately assured him that it had been nothing to do with him; and he said that in any case leaving home was the only thing I could have done.

In the meantime Jim and I were still looking for a boat; and during one of our working holidays in Ireland that we heard from the RNLI that the lifeboat from Troon was for sale. It was too late for us travel all the way up to the west coast of Scotland to inspect the boat before the tender date, but it seemed a shame to let the chance go by. We had already inspected the Coverack lifeboat down in Cornwall, but had failed to acquire it despite offering £1,200; so it was somewhat tongue-in-cheek that we put in an offer for the Troon boat of only £400. Much to our pleasure and surprise, it was accepted.

We re-named our new purchase *Venturer 2,* and its acquisition presented us with a fresh set of challenges. After inspecting and measuring this beautifully made and carefully maintained boat, we decided to change the propeller and to install a new Perkins L 4 M diesel engine. I had no previous experience of diesel engines, so I did a one-week course at Perkins of Peterborough to fill the gap in my knowledge.

The L 4 M was a new derivation from the standard L 4 engine that Perkins had manufactured for some time, but which they hadn't previously modified for use as a marine engine: hence the 'M' in L 4 M. They were therefore prepared to second their Mr. Galbraith to us for a week, because they were keen to obtain reports on how the engine performed. He joined us in Troon, where he helped to install the engine in *Venturer 2*, a process which included persuading the Troon shipyard to make two small but essential brackets. I then took her out as soon as I could, accompanied by the harbour-master, for a sea trial.

Inside the harbour, the water was deceptively calm; but, as we cleared the harbour wall and entered the Firth of Clyde, we met seas so violent that *Venturer 2* almost stood on end. I was taken completely unawares; but *Venturer 2* righted herself and her new engine worked beautifully. Once I had got her safely back into the harbour, Jim and I were able to leave our new boat in the safe hands of the harbour-master, confident that we had proved her worth, and our ability in what was for us a completely new field of engineering.

In August we returned to Scotland. First we spent a week in the east at the Edinburgh Festival, where we enjoyed a cultural feast, including a performance of Mozart's *The Magic Flute* and an excellent production of Dylan Thomas's magical *Under Milk Wood* with Donald Houston in the cast. Then, after watching the famous 'Edinburgh Tattoo' in the Castle forecourt, we travelled westward to Troon. There we boarded *Venturer 2* and brought her back to Aberdovey, calling in at Portpatrick in Wigtown, at Douglas on the Isle of Man, and at Holyhead on Holy Island, Anglesey. Fortunately our earlier lessons in navigation had not been forgotten and we had no problems finding these various ports.

Our only real difficulty was that Jim suffered from sea-sickness. However by trial and error we found both a liquid and a solid which his stomach could tolerate at sea; and from then on Martell's 5-star brandy and McVitie's digestive biscuits became standard ship's tack.

CHAPTER FIVE

World-wide events would now severely affect our business.

Back in 1952, the corrupt and corpulent King Farouk of Egypt had been compelled to abdicate within three days of a military coup; and by June 1956 Egypt had been transformed into a one-party socialist Arab state with Colonel Nasser as its President. The following month, however, Nasser announced that he had nationalised the Suez Canal Company, most of whose shares were held by the British Government. Our Prime Minister Sir Anthony Eden feared that Nasser would close the canal. So in November 1956, in secret alliance with Israel, and in open co-operation with France, he mounted an expedition with the object of taking control of the canal zone. However before the end of the year American pressure had obliged him to withdraw.

The 'Suez Crisis' as it was known had an immediate impact upon our business. By this time we were committed to the construction of a second filling station in the centre of Crewe. Half the money was to come from a marketing agreement with the Regent Oil Company; but on the outbreak of the crisis in July, their local representative visited us and told us quite casually that as a result of the uncertainty all marketing agreements had been suspended indefinitely.

Until this moment we had used our bank solely as somewhere to keep our money safe. So I was surprised as well as being relieved when I visited the bank manager to explain our difficulty and found him ready and willing to provide us with the funds we needed. This enabled us to go ahead with our development plans; and in July 1956 we opened the new premises in Badger Avenue, Crewe a street address we shared with the Rolls Royce works. Up until that time, we had been our own secretaries; but the pressure of work was now so great that we decided to appoint a full-time secretary. Fortunately Joan Agg was easy to find. We were now agents for most of the leading insurance and hire-purchase companies, and Joan was recruited from one of their offices in Shrewsbury.

Since our sales office at the 'Quick Service' filling station in Hope Valley was only twelve foot square, Joan Agg's appointment (followed by that of an 'office junior') meant that we needed additional office space, so we bought the wooden bungalow on the opposite side of the road. These premises would suffice for several years, until we built new offices and extended showrooms to accommodate our growing business.

That growth was sometimes dependent on chance. In 1957, for example, we were driving to London via Moreton-in-Marsh and Chipping Norton, when we happened to stop for petrol at Matthew Gold's Filling Station in Little Compton. It wasn't much to look at, but the site was good, and lo-and-behold Matthew was prepared to sell it to us for £1,650. We bought it, modernised the filling station and built a very attractive house. We then advertised for a Manager and had soon appointed Glyn Price from Llangurig, who moved into the new house with his wife and family.

The following year, 1958, we purchased the field opposite the Hope Valley Filling Station and put up a 6,000 sq. ft. Coseley industrial building, which provided us with generous workshop and showroom accommodation. This expansion was made possible by our having very fortunately secured the Morris and Morris Commercial Retail

'Before' and 'After' photos of the 'Quick Service Station' at Crewe

The 'Quick Service Station' in Hope Valley after 1954

dealership. This was entirely due to a chance meeting with the Mr. Roberts, the Sales Manager of 'Wales and Edwards', the Morris distributors. We had bought a Morris Ten which, quite by mistake, he had entered in a local motor auction with a price £100 less than it should have been. Roberts came to see that same evening and explained his error. When we allowed him to buy the car back from us at cost, he was overwhelmed with gratitude. "If there is ever anything I can do for you", he told us, "just let me know!" And it was that meeting which led to our Morris Agency.

By this time our office staff had grown to three, including Hilda Tipton our secretary, Hazel Williams our receptionist and telephonist, and Mrs. Beaton our book-keeper (who, with a name like hers, was inevitably though most unfairly teased about the dangers of 'cooking the books'); and we had as many as seven mechanics, who not only renovated our own vehicles, but also provided a repair service for retail customers, manned the petrol pumps and so on. This number of staff meant that we were increasingly tied down to routine management at the expense of our more entrepreneurial activities, which up to then had been exceptionally profitable. We kept our motor trade businesses for another seven years until 1965, and during that time we vastly increased their turnover. But the motor trade would never again be as happy and profitable to us as it had been in those exciting earlier days.

However, there were compensations. Some months after we had moved into our new offices, Hilda Tipton announced that she would be moving on, and so we advertised for a new secretary in the *Wellington Journal and Shrewsbury News*. Advertising had already played a significant part in developing our business and we had pioneered a number of innovative advertising ploys, which included inserting complete single

'Before' and 'After' photos of the 'Oil Well' filling station at Little Compton

Me in my late twenties with papers relating to the Morris Agency

columns of vehicles, and using photo-advertising to feature specific vehicles. Now a small classified advertisement costing just four-and-sixpence (4/6d) would dramatically change the course of my family history.

There was only one reply to our advert; but that was more than adequate, because it brought us Dorothy Poole from Shrewsbury. The two of us were soon sharing a comparatively small office, and it wasn't long before I was smitten. I remember that she was late for our first Sunday 'date', as the result of an argument with a 'No Waiting' sign on a Shrewsbury pavement. She had been driving a company car at the time, but this did nothing to spoil our day out. We drove into Wales and stopped for lunch at the Bear in Newtown. Wales at that time was still officially 'dry' on Sundays, but when we asked the proprietor if there was any chance of some wine with our lunch, he said that it would be all right provided that we chose white wine, and were prepared to drink it from lemonade glasses. We did and we were!

Once a month Dorothy and I travelled with Mrs. Beaton the book-keeper to our offices in Crewe, where we spent the day processing the whole of their credit accounts. This was an intensive piece of work which did not end until the accounts were all in stamped envelopes ready for posting. Afterwards, the art of the game lay in disposing of Mrs. Beaton, usually by putting her on a train back to Shrewsbury. Dorothy and I would then enjoy a candle-light dinner at Churches Mansion, where in those days an outstanding meal was served for seven-and-sixpence.

Dorothy had come for interview on 26 February 1959, and had started work on 9 March. By May I had proposed to her and had been accepted, and we were soon arranging our wedding for 24 October. We justified this early date to ourselves on the grounds that we didn't want Dorothy to have to travel all the way from Shrewsbury on the winter roads. My Mother, to whom we had given no explanation, wrote that she didn't understand why we had chosen such a dismal month, and added: 'Whatever are you going to do in the long winter evenings?' We decided not to enlighten her.

In the meantime, business was not all plain sailing. Back in 1958 the motor industry had been stimulated by the relaxation of controls on hire-purchase financing. Initially this had seemed most welcome, because it meant that we were allowed to accept a deposit of as little as 10%, with the balance to be repaid over as long as four years. However, all our HP financing was done on the basis of 'full recourse', which occasionally got us into difficulties. Just supposing that the buyer did not maintain his payments and also failed to look after the vehicle, this meant that it very quickly became worth less than the 90% which had been advanced to us — but we could be compelled by the hire purchase company to repossess the vehicle while paying them the full outstanding balance, including any unpaid interest. This only happened a few times, but when it did it was an unhappy as well as a deeply unprofitable operation.

Worse was to come. In July 1959 the new car market changed from being a sellers' market to a buyers' market for the first time since the end of World War II. Vauxhall built up a huge surplus of Victors and Veloxes, and in July they slashed their prices by 10% right across the board. This action not only brought prices down, but also upset the market and substantially reduced demand.

It would be twelve months before the market recovered. In the meantime we were fighting a losing battle. At the time, we realised that we were effectively working for nothing. With hindsight we reckoned that we had actually lost over £20,000, a substantial sum by any standards, and today's equivalent of at least £200,000.

So although I was very happy with Dorothy, it certainly wasn't 'roses, roses all the way'. Our wedding day couldn't come soon enough, and we were married at St. Chad's, the beautiful round church in the centre of Shrewsbury, with a big reception afterwards at the Britannia (now the Shrewsbury) Hotel.

After our honeymoon in Southern Ireland we returned to the bungalow which I had shared with Jim for the past eleven years. He had now moved out into a caravan which we had set up in the grounds; but he joined us for meals.

Dorothy and I had started our married life with three filling stations and the Morris Retail Agency, but with a substantial decline in the demand for first-class reconditioned second-hand cars, which had been our mainstay. We were therefore looking for fresh fields to conquer, and our first new venture was the establishment of 'Quick Service Van Hire Limited' (later abbreviated to 'Q Hire Limited'), our first independent limited company. The object of the company was to hire commercial vehicles on a self-drive basis. We had virtually no competition and the business took off very rapidly. It made economic sense because of our strong buying power, which meant that we could hire a vehicle for a whole season and still re-sell it for more than it had cost us initially. Neither Hertz nor Avis hired out vans, and we had soon extended our range from Morris 1000 and Morris Commercial Vans to Land-Rovers and 12- and 18-seater vehicles. Our customers included such big names as Rolls Royce and British Rail.

We were heavily involved in the new business when our neighbour Eric Hillage walked down and told us quite simply that he could no longer pay the wages needed to keep his stone transport business going. Would we pay him £150 for his lorry and the stone tips on his land? It was an offer we couldn't refuse. We ordered a new lorry, and had soon secured orders for loads of stone both from local builders and from the Forestry Commission.

We also found a special white spar stone in the tips, and sent samples of it to the Department of Scientific Industrial Research (DSIR). They came back to us very quickly with the welcome news that if we could wash and grade the product, they could almost certainly find us a ready market. So we installed hoppers and a triple screen washing plant in our old garage premises, which had become redundant. The DSIR were as good as their word and had soon put us in touch not only with Rowebbs of Glasgow, but also with other purchasers throughout England. What with the local road-stone and the washed and graded white spar stone, we had soon created a wonderful business. Indeed, the tremendous demand meant we had worked out most of the best material within five years, though the white spar tips continued to provide us with a modest income well into the 1990s.

However this success would be accompanied by the first major tragedy of my business career. It was 1963, and our driver Bill Lewis, a willing and likeable Cockney, had delivered a load of white spar chippings to South Wales. On his return journey in the early evening he was in a head-on collision with a lorry carrying a full load of concentrated hydrochloric acid in glass car-buoys. The car-buoys came over the top of the lorry cab, smashed through the windscreen of our vehicle and poured acid all over Bill Lewis, who died in hospital soon afterwards. There was little one could say to comfort his widow, and our vehicle was a write-off. As a result of this accident and several others of a similar nature, the regulations for carrying these dangerous liquids were tightened up; but it was too late to save poor Bill Lewis.

In the meantime, my first son Christopher had been born without complications on 7 November 1960 in Quarry Place Nursing Home, Shrewsbury, within a stone's throw of the church where Dorothy and I had been married. In anticipation of this event, and the fact that having children is bound to curtail one's freedom, we had already bought our first television set: black and white of course, because colour was not yet available, and with just two channels: BBC and ITV.

Christopher, usually known as Chris, made good use of the car showroom in his pram. Dorothy had been replaced as full-time Secretary first by her friend Betty Walsh, and then by Jone Wood, a great character who supported us through a difficult patch in our business; but she continued to work, and before he could even walk Chris was accompanying his mother while she collected and delivered cars from as far west as the Welsh coast and as far north as Liverpool.

It was at around this time that Glyn Price decided that he would like to go into business on his own behalf, and resigned as Manager of 'The Oil Well', our filling station at Little Compton. Jim, who had been fifty-four at the time of my marriage, felt that this would be an ideal opportunity for him to withdraw from the mainstream of the business; and he took over the 'Oil Well' as its owner-manager, living in the house we had built nearby. Sadly his health was failing, and it was not long before he sold up and moved to Ireland, where he purchased a cottage called Barnagearah, on a hill overlooking Bantry Bay. But he had hardly begun renovating Barnagearah when he tried to help a stranger whose car had become stuck on the hill. Tragically the effort was too much for him, and he collapsed and died with a coronary heart attack. Dorothy and I travelled over to his funeral in Ireland.

First as Eric Rance, and then as Jim Manson, he had been an exceptionally good friend to me for 27 years, setting me an example that I have tried to emulate and been proud to follow. I missed him very much indeed, though the shock was naturally cushioned a little by his having already left the business, and by the fact that I had my growing family around me, my second son Philip having been born on 2 November 1962.

In the meantime, despite the fact that we were busy enough with the fairly substantial business we already had, Dorothy and I had founded RJ and DE Freeman Transport Contracts. We then purchased four lorries, engaged drivers, and sent them up under contract to work on the Treweryn Dam. This proved to be a mistake. The rates were highly uncompetitive, conditions were abysmal, and the problems of vehicle maintenance and of staff seemed to be never-ending. We closed the business down and sold the vehicles within six months, counting ourselves fortunate to have burnt our fingers only slightly.

From that time on, as our business continued to grow, we never seemed to be far away from solicitors and accountants. My apologies for the cancerous simile, but over the years they have ranged from the positively benign to the vilely malignant. Among our solicitors, I have already mentioned dear John Yates (who guided us with so much understanding from 1954-1986); but at various times in the past Jim and I had also suffered from the incompetent Mr. Bourlay, the corrupt Mr. Nettleton and the delightful but eccentric Mr. O'Mahoney.

Bourlay, gangling and bespectacled, seemed like a figure from a Dickens novel. Never did a man seem to do so much, and yet achieve so little.

Nettleton had been given the job of converting the original partnership between Jim and myself into the limited company A.J. Manson Ltd, which is now the holding company of our group. The actual forming of the company was carried out expeditiously. Not long afterwards however, as a result of various transactions, we were owed a substantial sum by an oil company. Despite repeated assurances from the oil company that the cheque had been posted, it never came to hand. Then we discovered that it had been sent to Mr. Nettleton, upon whom we had to exert considerable pressure before he eventually disgorged what was due to us. A year or two later, learning that Nettleton had just been sent to prison for embezzling clients' funds, we realised that we had had a narrow escape

O'Mahoney was the hale and hearty Irish solicitor whose job it had been to convey Kate O'Leary's cottage to us. A most congenial 'pat-on-the-back' type of Irishman, the only thing he kept forgetting to do was any of the relevant paperwork. Every time we went over to Ireland we paid O'Mahoney a visit, and it was always: "To be sure, Mr. Freeman, 'tis all in order, dese t'ings take a dale of toime. Niver you worry a bit, Oi'll say to everytin". After three years we still had no documentary proof of ownership, and turned in desperation to John Yates, who sent O'Mahoney a strong letter before our next visit. Within weeks the matter was concluded; and we were more than glad of it, for on our next visit but one we discovered that O'Mahoney had upped and gone, and to the best of our knowledge he was never seen again.

The accountants have also been a mixed bunch. We are now fortunate enough to be dealing with Dennis Muxworthy and Roger Parkes, excellent men with a sound understanding of our business; and in the early days we had a twenty-year association with the worthy Mr. Holyoak, who seemed old and weary to me when I first met him in 1950, but was still looking after other people's accounts more than forty years later. In between, however, we were not always so fortunate.

There was Keith Winter, for example. We met him as a result of a brief partnership entered into by Mr. Holyoak, and he seemed at that time to answer all our needs. However he handled our accounts in such an un-businesslike manner that he involved us in a completely unnecessary tax inquiry which cost us many thousands of pounds; and at about that time he was involved within his practice in some sort of a scandal which meant that he had to leave at a moment's notice.

After a relatively tranquil interim, we were then introduced, unfortunately for us, to Mr Ingram Legge.

Mr. Legge promised us the earth, but (not surprisingly, perhaps) failed to deliver. As a side-line, he also became one of the Directors of a company in which we were jointly involved. But when all that company's considerable resources had been absorbed in consultancy fees, transport charges and accountancy charges, it suddenly transpired that his position within his firm made it impossible for him to remain on the Board. So he resigned, leaving us with a company with substantially more liabilities than assets. Fortunately this turned out to be the proverbial darkest hour before the dawn, because it was after this that we were introduced to Dennis Muxworthy and Roger Parkes.

Long before that time, back in early 1963, Dorothy and I were thinking seriously about our housing problem: the fact that the Runnis bungalow simply wasn't large enough for a growing family. At first we thought of extending our bungalow, and we even asked an architect to draw up some plans. However by the time the plans were ready we had decided that it would make more sense to make a complete move. We weren't sure exactly what we were looking for, but we felt that we would recognise it when we saw it; and we began spending one afternoon or evening a week house-hunting.

It was not until the summer of 1963 that a large house on the eastern fringe of Shrewsbury came onto the market. Pimley Manor, as it was called, was already known to Dorothy, who had frequently passed it when she was in her teens; and we obtained the particulars and arranged to view the property. The door of this imposing 1849 brick-built mansion was opened to us by wee Mrs. Campbell, sister-in-law of the redoubtable Miss Campbell who had lived there alone for twenty-seven years after her mother's death. Mrs. Campbell seemed to like us, and to be willing us to buy the property, though we had soon realised that it was far too large.

Outside, there were seven acres of grounds, so overgrown that it was virtually impossible to assess what was there. There were also stables, a lodge, a summer house, a games room, a dairy, a potting shed, an ancient system for pumping water, and a rudimentary electrical installation dating from 1936. We tried to count the number of rooms as we went round, but lost track somewhere in the fifties. The house had originally contained fourteen 'inside' servants, one or more of whom could be summoned using a bell system which serviced virtually every room. There was also

Pimley Manor from the air

an antiquated and hopelessly inadequate central heating system, consisting of five radiators in the hall and landing serviced by a vast coke stove in the corner of the kitchen.

But despite its size and the fact that it was very run-down, we had fallen in love with Pimley Manor. We knew that it was to be sold by auction on the first Tuesday in August; and on our way home, as we weighed up the possibilities, we thought that it would probably go for a figure that would be way beyond our means. However, we decided to put in a bid.

On the day of the sale, there was a marquee in front of the house, with furniture all around (the furniture was to be sold immediately after the house had been auctioned); and there were crowds of people everywhere. Looking up at the Manor House, it seemed ridiculous that we should be even contemplating such a purchase. And then the bidding began. It opened at £5,000. After only my third bid, no-one was prepared to go any higher. The auctioneer brought his hammer down with a loud thud, and Pimley Manor was ours for £7,000. We hadn't yet found all the money, but the die was cast.

Once again we had been fortunate. That very evening we were telephoned by the agents offering us an immediate profit of £1,500. It appeared that one of the prospective purchasers had sent a representative to bid on his behalf at the sale, but had given him an inadequate limit, and then gone racing. Their loss was our gain. The offer, worth well over £15,000 in today's terms, was certainly a tempting one, but we had no difficulty in turning it down.

There was one slightly curious aftermath. John Yates, who did the legal paperwork for us, had never lived in Shrewsbury himself; but his family home had originally been what is now the Convent in College Hill, and he said to me: "Wasn't there supposed to be a 'White Lady' who haunted the place? I seem to remember being told something when I was a lad."

CHAPTER SIX

It was on 14 December 1963, just four hectic months after my successful bid for Pimley Manor, that Dorothy and I and three-year-old Christopher and one-year-old Philip moved in. We brought with us Sally, the German Shepherd whom I had already begun to regard as the children's nanny. In fact she protected whichever child was in the pram so ferociously that I would later be hauled into court for being the owner of a dog that was not under proper control!

By this time our heating expert (alarmingly named Mr. Frost) had installed an up-to-date oil-fired central heating system; and we had made four or five rooms basically habitable: a living room, the kitchen, two bedrooms and a new bathroom.

When we finally got to bed that first night Dorothy and I were very tired. But we were woken at about 3 a.m. by a dreadful wind and whistling in the chimney.

"I am sure I can hear someone walking about upstairs", my wife said, so I went to investigate. Opening one of the upper rooms, I found myself in the presence of a trim and beautiful lady, dressed all in white, and immediately John Yates's words came back to me. Curiously I didn't feel at all frightened. We even had a kind of conversation, though I don't remember what was said, except that after a while the White Lady intimated that she must be going because it was late. She then disappeared through a little door, which was rather like one of the doors in *Alice in Wonderland*.

When I investigated the next morning, I found a trap door in the little room behind;

Philip and Christopher with a repentant Sally

Picture: Shropshire Star

and Dorothy would later insist on having the trap door sealed up. In due course I also looked into the history of the White Lady. The story was that the first occupants of Pimley Manor had been a mother and her 20-year-old daughter, who became known locally as 'the White Lady' since she was invariably dressed in white, rode side-saddle on a white horse which she kept in a white stable — and so on and so forth. At any rate, she had suddenly disappeared. The rumour was that she had run away with a businessman who was thought to be quite 'unsuitable' for someone of her rank in society. Since then, she had been seen on a number of occasions either in the grounds, or at one of the windows of the house. Perhaps things had worked out badly for her in the outside world, and she had returned in death to the place she had most loved in life.

At the time, any worries about the supernatural were rapidly overtaken by more down-to-earth concerns: the first of which was a very happy one. Only three days after our arrival, Sally gave birth in the washroom to thirteen healthy pups.

The next concern was financial. We urgently needed more income to run our large establishment (how inadequate the furniture from our two-bed-roomed bungalow had seemed when it was unloaded at Pimley from the back of one of our lorries), and we thought there was no reason why the Manor should not help to pay for itself.

Some of the buildings had already been turned into individual living areas. Over a period of time we refurbished and reorganised these to create five flats named after five trees: Oak, Beech, Pine, Poplar and Ash. We also converted the dairy premises into what we called the 'Mews', and the Lodge was divided into two. This made a total of eight new homes each of which, fully furnished, brought us in six guineas (£6/6s/0d) per week.

Furnishing these premises meant attending numerous furniture auctions, something we thoroughly enjoyed; while building them and fitting them out involved us with a number of interesting characters. These included Fred Childs, who worked like a demon provided that he was too far away from a licensed premises to be able to reach it in his lunch hour; Jack Hayes, a most competent plumber, who worked for us on and off for twenty-five years, though he grew slower and slower until he virtually came to a stand-still; his brother Ken, an exceptionally good electrician; and Norman Owen, a wonderful joiner. Norman's only drawback was that he was a great worrier. "The work'll come to an end one day", he was always saying, "and then I'll be out of a job, you'll see!" As it turned out, our work has never come to an end, so he could have saved himself several decades of constant anxiety.

It turned out to be a good time to be offering furnished accommodation. This was partly because Kenya had been granted independence in December 1963 with my former companion Jomo Kenyatta as its first Prime Minister. He turned out to be a very successful leader, but at the time many white people, fearing for their future, had returned to England at short notice and needed somewhere to live.

Once we had completed all the Pimley flats we decided to continue in this new direction, and so we purchased the Vicarage and Verger's Cottage at 15 Mount Street, Shrewsbury. These we converted into eight flats which (once again following my preference for names over numbers) we called Church, Chapel, Minster, Cathedral, Priory, Abbey, Vicarage and Rectory.

15 Mount Street

The expertise I was gaining in the course of fitting out all these flats would soon be put to good use in another related field.

It all began with our founding in mid-1963 of Shilphone Agricultural Ltd., with the aim of employing a manager, together with drivers and a small fleet of lorries, to buy root crops, hay and straw in fertile East Anglia, and sell them into Shropshire and Central Wales. As an idea it had sounded simple and straightforward; but unfortunately the manager's confidence exceeded his competence, the sellers' and buyers' ideas about what constituted high quality did not appear to coincide, and there were times when we found ourselves in the fields hastily loading bales of hay and straw in a desperate effort to outwit the vagaries of the British climate. The business, as you may have gathered, was not an unqualified success, and we felt obliged to put it into voluntary liquidation. The creditors castigated us severely, but things could have been worse, and we did succeed in paying them twelve-and-sixpence in the pound.

It was also the Shilphone affair which first drew us to the attention of Lynn Dewing, who lived and farmed on three hundred acres at Ampthill in Bedfordshire. Lynn ran a business which was similar to ours, though on a substantially larger scale, and seemed to us to be in a league of his own. Besides his farm, he owned a yacht in the Mediterranean, he thought nothing of flying to Paris for a race meeting, and he always travelled (frequently with an attractive woman described as his 'secretary') in a nearly new Jaguar. He thought nothing of opening the boot of this prestigious car to reveal what was clearly an expensive oil painting — such paintings being another commodity in which he evidently dabbled.

Now it happened that Lynn had bought a Shropshire property, namely the redundant buildings of Condover Airfield. However, he was perennially short of ready money, and he was looking for someone willing to pay £2,000 to acquire a 50% stake in the property, and then to help him develop and manage it. It didn't take us long to decide that we would go in with him.

In the early stages, Lynn was a reasonably active business partner, helping to put a chain-link fence around the property, and installing a comprehensive water supply system. After that it was pretty well left to me to renovate the buildings, instal toilet facilities, find tenants and produce leases. My greatest challenge on the site was an old aircraft hanger, which would need an expensive new roof before it could be let. I decided that it would be most unlikely that this large property would be wanted by a local tenant, so I gambled on a single advertisement in *The Daily Telegraph*. This produced just two replies, but one of them was soon translated into a tenancy which lasted over twenty-two years; and much to my delight, the first two quarters of rent paid for the new roof.

Another business venture was not so successful. We had hoped to extend our Q-Hire business, using the stables at Pimley Manor as the base for a parcel delivery service. We were convinced that many local suppliers needed a more reliable and economic transport service: many of them were using rural bus services to deliver their goods! So we began with a fleet of vans painted in a fine new livery, and a band of women drivers wearing a smart uniform of white overall and red beret. Sadly we were ahead of our time; we could not persuade enough people to change their business practices; and since we could not risk incurring losses for any considerable time, we

Stonehurst, 24 Sutton Road, which we converted into 14 flats in 1965

'Before' and 'After' photos of unit 86 on the Condover Industrial Estate

reluctantly called it a day, paid off our staff and sold off our vehicles. Fortunately the remainder of the Q-Hire business was going from strength to strength.

In May 1964 our third son Jonathan was born at Pimley Manor; and as I drove to fetch the nurse, I became aware for a few minutes that the White Lady was sitting in the car beside me. Once again, it was not at all a frightening experience.

Since we were now involved not only in our two filling stations and our commercial vehicle hire, but also in flat development and in commercial estates, we were in danger of becoming over-extended.

Fortunately our marketing contract with our petrol suppliers for Crewe Filling Station was due to run out in 1965, and the site had become extremely successful. The happy result was that during the summer and autumn of 1964 we had visits by appointment from representatives of every major petrol company, including our own suppliers, all of them wanting us to sell. So we held an auction; and although we had been 'playing hard to get', when the bidding reached more than two-and-a-half times the opening bid, we decided that it was time to accept. In the words of 'Take Your Pick' one of the first and the most popular of all the quiz shows, we said to ourselves: "Don't open the box take the money!" And having decided to sell up at Crewe, we also marketed our small filling station at Minsterley. The result was that while we were both still comparatively young, Dorothy and I had money in hand.

It was a very good thing that we were now free of the responsibility of garages and workshops and petrol retailing. Not only had these involved us in businesses which were open for twelve hours a day, seven days a week; but also we had had to cope with constant stress both from trying to control cash and credit, and from staffing problems. In only eleven years, for example, we had had eight filling station managers, of whom only two had distinguished themselves: Mick Johnson and Glyn Price, both of whom I have already mentioned. Mick not only created the business at Crewe virtually from scratch, but was later (after a period away from the company) a pillar of strength on maintenance; while Glyn did a similarly good job at Little Compton, later came to Shrewsbury as our Transport Manager, and subsequently ran his own business distributing pet food from premises rented from us. Mick has remained a life-long friend; while Glyn very sadly died in harness while still far too young.

The date for the completion of the sale of the Crewe filling station was 1 January 1965; and then it seemed more fortunate than ever that the sale had gone through, because on that very day I went down with pneumonia. The situation was aggravated by the fact that our regular doctor was unavailable, and a locum failed to diagnose how serious was my condition. Dorothy, at her wits' end, and realising how ill I was, persuaded another doctor to call on a Sunday. He took one look at me and within a few minutes I was being carried out of the house to a waiting ambulance in which I was whisked away to hospital.

I was so ill that I experienced the symptoms related by many others who have been close to death: that is, the whole of my past life seemed to pass before me. Once again, I saw my sisters go off to school and longed to join them. Once again I was terrified in Grandma's house by a reproduction of Holman Hunt's *The Light of the World*. "I know who he is!" declared Miss Nix fiercely. "And he knows who he is! He had better come to my study straight after assembly." There was the Silver Jubilee Procession of

King George V and Queen Mary passing below the window; and there was the bucket which needed filling with stones in the garden of our new house at Sewardstonebury. Things went faster and faster after that: I saw Eric Rance again working on his chicken-farm; German and English aeroplanes wheeled and circled above my head; I collected all my worldly goods and cycled away in the direction of Birmingham; Jim and I were sailing through stormy waters off the Welsh coast; there was Dorothy coming in for her interview on that very first meeting; and then I knew nothing more until I came to myself lying peacefully but feeling very weak in a hospital bed in the Royal Salop Infirmary in the middle of Shrewsbury.

My stay in this large but neglected Georgian building, built back in 1826, was a fairly extended one; and altogether I was out of commission for two or three months. Fortunately Dorothy was the proverbial tower of strength. During my illness and convalescence she took over complete responsibility not only for our home and family, but also for the whole of our business interests, which included managing a great deal of property as well as overseeing the Q-Hire operation.

Q-Hire now had a fleet which during the winter months consisted of around sixty vehicles, increasing to nearer one hundred in the summer. It contained a wide variety of vehicles, ranging from Morris Minis, Morris 1100s and Ford Cortina saloons, to Ford Escort and Transit Vans (both 12-and 18-seaters) and Land Rovers. Most of the fleet was out on long-term contract hire, with only a small proportion on weekly or weekend hiring.

The Shropshire base for Q-Hire had been relocated to Pimley Manor once we had sold the garages. In this way we made good use of the stables and coach house, where John Lockley and his assistant Malcolm presided over our maintenance facilities. There were occasional black days, but not many. Once, for example, a Mini was not returned. Potentially we stood to lose a great deal of money. Eventually, in frustration, I put a small classified advertisement in both *The Daily Mail* and *The Daily Express*. The result was that an elderly clergyman rang up from Portsmouth, saying that he thought he knew where our car was to be found. John Lockley was promptly despatched and much to our relief he recovered the car.

As for the Crewe branch: towards the end of 1965 we moved it into newly acquired premises consisting of a yard and a shop with a flat above, on the corner of Market Street and Wrexham Terrace. This was the scene of what could have been a major family tragedy.

Cups of tea had been sent down from the flat to the shop; and my three-year-old son Philip was returning the empty cups to the flat, using an outside staircase. But the stair-rails were too widely spaced, and Philips's hands were full; and when he tripped he fell right through them. All I heard was a terrible thud, and I rushed out to find him an unconscious heap on the ground. I picked him up, and was later told that it was only the speed with which we got him to Queen Alexandra Hospital that saved his life. Philip had a fractured skull and severe concussion.

We were told that we must try and somehow get through to him, and make him recognise us and respond to us. I remembered that Philip was amused by one of the family jokes, which was that although Dad enjoyed singing and sang a great deal, it was always in his own special way, as Dad couldn't really sing at all. So I concentrated on this with all my power, singing and joking about my singing, until at last to my intense relief Philip nodded his head, indicating that I had got through to him and he was sharing my joke.

Philip was in hospital for another three weeks, and for most of that time either Dorothy or I was with him. When he was allowed home, we were told that he would have to be very carefully treated for at least six months. That became a very happy time for me, because from then until he was ready to start school Philip began accompanying me on all my visits to industrial estates, building sites and so on. Not only did this create a special bond between us, but also Philip met most of the people involved in the business. I like to think that this is what laid the foundation of his interest in the company and its works, an interest which blossomed so magnificently that as I write these words my dear son Philip is the Managing Director of the whole company.

Financially, purchase of those premises in Crewe turned out to be particularly advantageous. Within a few months of acquiring them and moving in, I was telephoned out of the blue by a Crewe solicitor. He was winding up the estate of a lady who had recently died, and who had owned seven of the adjoining properties. "Would you be interested in buying them?" he asked.

"We could be", I replied cautiously. "What price are you thinking of?"

"£3,500."

"You've got yourself a deal."

They were tenanted terraced houses, and at first little could be done with them. But 'nothing venture, nothing gain', as the saying goes; and over the years whenever we had the opportunity we bought further houses in the block.

In the meantime the Q-Hire business continued to be profitable. The only complication was that there was a regular need to transfer vehicles between the Crewe and Shrewsbury branches. Fortunately our gardener at Pimley Manor, George Gollins, was able to double up as a driver. George, incidentally, had a rather particular claim to fame, in that he had invented a beet-hoeing machine designed to be towed behind a tractor, and capable of hoeing six rows of beet at the same time. I never saw the machine itself, but I did see George's photographs of this formidable-looking machine with its copious quantity of pedals and levers. Sadly for George, it was not commercially viable. The problem was that not only did it require a man to drive the tractor, but six more men, one to each row, to operate the pedals and levers. Still, it was fortunate for us, because George Gollins was a good man and he stayed with us as a gardener and driver for many years.

CHAPTER SEVEN

The drawing-room at Pimley Manor after restoration

Our lovely home at Pimley Manor became a source of more and more pleasure. Inside, we continued a process of careful restoration. Outside, using a Land Rover and chains to clear the undergrowth, we were constantly discovering new features in the grounds. At the bottom of the field, for example, there stood a row of Poplars which Mr Perks, the tree man, said were the largest he had ever seen. Since they were blocking our view of Haughmond Hill, we sold him the trees for a substantial sum and used the money for a great deal of new planting. This included more poplars and also a large number of conifers. The conifers we doubled up, planting them 2'6" apart, both in the grounds of Pimley Manor and on other miscellaneous pieces of land we had acquired here and there. This resulted in quite a nice little earner for a number of years at Christmas-time; and at Pimley itself, the trees which remain after thirty years of thinning form quite a substantial stand.

Keeping an eye on the Q-Hire business, we had noticed that most of our 12- and 18-seater vehicles were being hired by schools, scout groups and the like, in many cases for visits to the continent. We began to think that this was an area of our business which we could profitably develop, especially as Kate and Jack Myddle, who had originally joined us as managers of the Crewe Q-Hire operation and the Crewe filling station, had experience of running a Travel Agents.

Now I mentioned that the Market Street property which we had acquired in Crewe towards the end of 1965 had included a small shop; and we decided that we could turn this into a Travel Agents. So we applied to the Association of British Travel Agents (ABTA) for membership, only to be promptly turned down. However, we were told that we could appeal, so appeal we did; and in due course we were informed that our case would be heard in London, at the ABTA Headquarters near Euston Station.

Dorothy and I had no idea what to expect, and did not use a solicitor to represent us. We simply travelled down to London on the appointed day and appeared before a kind of Court, in which everything was done with great formality. Eventually the moment came for me to stand up and put my case. I'm not sure to this day how I managed to convince them; but the result was that our appeal was successful, and ABTA gave us the right to trade as Travel Agents: which we did.

In time there were further developments in Crewe, where there were now only a couple of houses on our block that we did not own. Before long we were able to put in a planning application to Crewe Council, seeking permission to build a new hotel on the site. Although they seemed extremely helpful, they couldn't bring themselves to a definite 'yes' or a definite 'no', and after a long while it turned out that although they would like us to build an hotel, they thought they had a better site. Would we be interested in a site swap? We said that we would; but once again we found ourselves involved in a long delay and considerable expense. Eventually I went to see the Crewe Planning Officer, and put it to him that whatever happened in the future, he now had a moral obligation to grant us the planning consent for which we had applied on our original site. He agreed and the planning consent was granted.

Then within a matter of months there were major changes to the Crewe Town Plan. These involved a major road going straight through part of the site on which we now had planning permission for an hotel. Crewe Council therefore had no option but to ask us to sell the site to them. This we did, and we were very glad to do so. Our resources would not really have stretched to building an hotel in Crewe, and in any case we had other fish to fry.

In the meantime we used the profits from this transaction to buy Brooklyn House in Crewe as a new base for our hiring operation. Brooklyn House, a large derelict doctor's house and surgery, had soon been converted into three shops, two suites of offices, and a yard and premises for Q-Hire. We let and managed the shops and offices for many years, disposing of them only when our other interests in Crewe were sold.

Coming back to 1966, the most outstanding event of the year so far as I was concerned was the birth on 11 July of our fourth child. Again I was aware that Pimley Manor's resident ghost was accompanying me in my car on my way to fetch the mid-wife. The White Lady seemed happier than I had ever known her; and a few hours later Janet Elizabeth was born, our only daughter. Dorothy and I might have gone on to have more children; but we both thought that four made a good-sized family. After all, the average was already down to 2.4 children and falling; and so I went on to have a vasectomy. I felt some trepidation about this operation, but can assure any similarly anxious male readers that it made everything even better than before.

Having sold the garages, we had decided that our policy would be to concentrate upon renting, hiring or leasing services; and towards the end of 1966 I saw a small advertisement in *The Sunday Times,* introducing to the UK a new American security system which involved close-circuit television and time-lapse camera. If we decided to become involved, this would fit in with our policy, because Photoscan was looking for distributors who would lease security equipment: so Dorothy and I went down to a presentation which had been arranged at the Hilton Hotel in London. We were

'Before' and 'After' photos of Brooklyn House in Crewe

thoroughly impressed by what we learned from the Photoscan team led by Ron Hibbard and Val Barber; and it did not take us long to decide that we should like to acquire three of their principal areas in the Midlands and the North.

The only problem was that we needed to make an investment of £16,500 cash down, which meant that we needed to borrow £12,000 from the Bank. Unfortunately the new manager at our own bank turned us down flat. However, having spent the rest of the morning touring the other clearing banks in Shrewsbury I soon had several offers of the necessary finance, and I chose to accept the one made by Martin's Bank — not long before it was taken over by Barclays.

Our deal with Photoscan included training in the intricacies of their system; so in January 1967 Dorothy and I went down to London again for a one-week training course run by George Faith at the Mount Royal Hotel. We also met our fellow distributors who had acquired the southern areas: a mixed bunch of people ranging from Stanley Cook, who had worked for Mappin and Webb; to Jo Lys, a returning tea planter. What united us was our enthusiasm and our determination to make the project succeed. We also shared the feeling that the training was on the thin side; but we later realised that George Faith had done the best job he could in what were fairly difficult circumstances.

The training course over, we returned to Shrewsbury to put what we had learned into practice. However, the English retailers did not welcome us with open arms in the way in which (we were told) the Americans had. It was difficult trying to convince not only managers but also their boards of directors that they needed our services, which would involve them in spending thousands of pounds over a three year period. For five months Dorothy and I and our three representatives Mike Maddox, Geoff Sledge and Don Lehmann worked hard without achieving a single order.

Don, incidentally, only worked hours to suit himself, and directed his efforts mainly at the National Coal Board, where the scope for installing CCTV systems was potentially vast. As for Mike and Geoff: I would go out with them one at a time, and we would divide a town east/west or north/south and go to work, agreeing to meet at a cafe for lunch.

At last, in May, we obtained our first order. It was only for one 'unit', to cover a very small jewellers in Union Street, Birmingham; but we were overjoyed. Within a few weeks we had an order for two 'units' from a Co-op in Manchester, and several more began trickling in.

The real turning-point, however, came when in the middle of one morning I took a telephone call from the Chief Security Officer of *C&A Modes*. "I'm very interested in your equipment", he told me. "Can one of your men meet me at our Coventry branch this afternoon?"

"By a coincidence", I said, "I shall be in Coventry myself this afternoon." Naturally I didn't tell him that I was the only person who could possibly be there! "Shall I meet your train?"

I did; and fortunately the CSO had obviously had a fairly generous liquid lunch on the train. This made him slightly aggressive, but comparatively easy to deal with. That is to say, he didn't appear to notice any of the massive gaps in my knowledge. I was totally ignorant of the environment of such a large store, and yet I was doing my best to make a thorough survey prior to quoting for installation of our equipment. Somehow or other I passed muster; because the CSO not only ordered installations to be made in six of the company's largest stores, but also promised that if within six months our installation had justified its costs, he would make further orders.

In due course he was as good as his word. After six months, computer printouts were prepared for the C&A Head Office giving the relevant 'shrinkage' figures; and according to those figures our installations had already saved them some £154,000.

One part of the Photoscan work which I didn't enjoy was giving presentations myself; and my very first experience of having to stand up and talk to a large audience was a particularly daunting one. We had been asked by the Cheshire Constabulary whether we could send an expert to their Chester headquarters to talk to a security seminar. This time I was the expert. I prepared copious notes, but the aura of a lecture theatre was new to me. Moreover, it was completely packed with police officers of all ranks, ranging from constables up to assistant chief constables. I never really learned what they thought of my performance, but I went home mentally and physically exhausted, and I had to spend the next day in bed.

I also made two visits to the head offices of Boots in Nottingham. The first was to their original offices in the centre of the city, where I talked about Photoscan to a small group of directors and senior personnel. Although once again well-prepared, I suffered the traumatic experience of completely drying up. In retrospect this probably wasn't for long, but at the time it seemed like an eternity. In fact far from damaging our prospects, my drying-up led to my receiving more sympathetic consideration once I was all right again. My second visit was to their new offices on the outskirts of Nottingham, where visitors approach the imposing premises through carefully landscaped green fields. The inside struck me as a Cathedral among offices, a kind of temple to efficiency. I entered through vast doors into an open-plan nave, divided into areas only by minimal 5 ft acoustic screens. Only the most senior incumbents were allowed their own private retreats on the periphery of this vast expanse; and in one of those retreats I was served tea with a silver service. Although I did not bring away an order that day, I had laid the foundation for the substantial business which Photoscan would do with *Boots* in subsequent years.

We also mounted and manned a number of exhibitions in co-operation with Photoscan London: a job which I hated. We did one exhibition in Scotland and two in London, one at the Lancaster Hotel and the other at Earls Court.

We were then asked to support the German Franchise holder who was putting on an exhibition in Cologne. By that time, Photoscan had produced a machine which could be used for relaying advertising information onto television screens within a store. By today's standards it was a fairly crude machine; and although it looked impressive, it was far too large to be hidden away in a suitcase, so I was nervous that there might be a problem going through the German customs at Cologne. However, Karl Dickerhoff told me not to worry; and he was as good as his word. He was there personally at the customs barrier. Ignoring the customs officers, he simply went round behind them and, much to my relief, took the equipment from me. A hectic few days followed: German hospitality was generous; the speed on the German autobahns was frightening at times; and I had never seen an exhibition on the scale of the one in Cologne. It occupied fourteen interconnected exhibition halls.

My other presentations included one at the head office of Samuels the jewellers in Birmingham, an unsuccessful visit made more irritating by the fact that I managed to lock my car key inside my car. On another occasion I spent an agreeable week at Newmarket trying to persuade the stables to make use of our surveillance equipment. Despite considerable interest, no orders followed. As so often happened, we were ahead of our time and that particular market was not yet ready for us.

Fortunately there were better days. I remember one in particular when I picked up two firm orders in Leicester, one of them from Asda; and I spent that night at the best hotel in Hull where, dining alone in the restaurant, I had veal marsala prepared at my table. Having carefully noted both the ingredients and the method of preparation, I subsequently astonished Dorothy, who had become used to my lack of culinary expertise, by cooking the same dish at home.

Still more productive was a visit to *Cleopatra's Palace,* an exotic new nightclub in Newport, which came complete with a casino, a dining area and live shows. The proprietor, a large thick-set Maltese, told us as he dabbed the sweat from his neck and forehead, that he wanted to be able to view everything in the club from the privacy of his personal sanctum. "Everything?" we enquired.

"Everything! On the dance-floor, I want to see who dances with who. In the kitchen, if they are working or not! But most important, the gaming tables. Not just a general view, you understand. I want to see every move the croupiers make!"

We had never done an installation of this nature before, and we were careful not to burn our fingers by under-pricing. We worried that we might be endangering the order; but although the Maltese mopped a little more sweat from his neck, he never blinked an eyelid. In fact he was so pleased with the final installation and the way it fitted into the red plush and gold of his club, that he made Dorothy and me life members.

Although *Cleopatra's Palace* was somewhat alien to us, we went along once, so as not to appear ungrateful. And then within months the whole place was totally destroyed by a vast fire. We of course were fully insured for the loss of our equipment. But we never saw the large Maltese again. We assumed that he too was properly insured.

By now we had two permanent staff on the technical and installation side of the business: Dennis Pye, and Ken Hayes whom I have already mentioned as an exceptionally good electrician. Unfortunately these two installation engineers usually had to work at night, which meant that the firm was in effect operating a 24-hour day. Any problems they encountered would be beamed back to base, where we depended upon the electronic expertise of Philip Briggs. Annoyingly they had problems a-plenty, because much of the Photoscan equipment which arrived from the USA was hopelessly sub-standard. Worst of all were the time-lapse cameras, which were then the only realistic tool for making permanent surveillance records, because video-recording was in its infancy and far too expensive.

Despite grandiose promises from Photoscan's head office in Los Angeles about technical support (we had been told about a 'technical division', and reference had also been made to their factories, including one in Kowloon), extensive correspondence produced almost nothing worthwhile. I was in touch with Peter Goddard, the leader of Photoscan London, who had experienced the same problems; and eventually he and I decided that in October 1967 we would fly out to Los Angeles to confront the senior management.

Up to that time, the furthest place to which I had flown was Ireland, so the flight first across the North Pole and then right across America was for me an outstanding experience. Formally entering the USA was not so agreeable. The problem was that Ron Hibbard had asked me to bring back four very expensive but defective Rolex cameras for repair, and they were safely tucked away in the bottom of my suitcase. But when we had stepped off the aeroplane and arrived among the last four or five in the customs hall, I realised that everyone ahead of us was having their cases searched. It seemed inevitable that the cameras would be found, and I had not brought adequate paperwork with me to account for them. Slowly the vast queue moved forward, and the moment when I would be arrested for smuggling crept steadily closer. Finally it was my turn — and then to my delight the last five of us were waved through!

However Photoscan Los Angeles was a severe disappointment. Its headquarters was a corridor of rented offices; and its much-vaunted technical department was not much more than a cupboard at the end of that corridor. The Photoscan hierarchy, consisting chiefly of Ron Hibbard, Val Barber and George Faith, did their best to take our minds off the obvious inadequacies of their business by taking us out on the town to fancy restaurants and night-clubs.

We went to the *Luan* restaurant, for example, a stylish place which offered us tasters of every main course before we had to choose what we wanted. The *Luan* had an Hawaiian theme: there was a stream running through the middle of the dining-room and a full-sized Hawaiian canoe suspended from the ceiling. The outstanding feature of another place — I forget the name, perhaps because I had drunk more than usual — was a pianist playing at an exceptionally large white grand piano. Then there was *Diamond Jim's,* with its bright red buttoned-leather upholstery, and its apparently limitless supply of hard liquor.

Our outings weren't entirely confined to the evenings. For example, Peter Goddard had a burning desire to visit a topless bar, and I wasn't averse to joining him. So in the middle of one morning we went to a topless bar and drank our beers while a semi-naked woman went through her usual languid routine. It was a novelty, but much less entertaining than I had been led to believe.

Our return flight was uneventful. Peter and I both had to face the unpalatable truth that from now on, so far as technical expertise was concerned, we were very much on our own. However, any sense of disappointment I felt personally was more than balanced by the sheer delight of being reunited with Dorothy.

Over the next four years we continued to make steady progress with our Photoscan operation, and there were several staff changes. Geoff Sledge was a hard worker and a man of shining integrity, but he was not persuasive enough as a salesman, and he sensibly returned to the Property Services Agency from where he had originally come. Don Lehmann also left us. He had never been very fully involved; though he felt hard done by after he had gone when Mike Maddox, building on Don's groundwork, secured substantial orders from the National Coal Board and took both the credit and the commission.

The addition to our Photoscan team was John Hanrahan. Following his father's example, John had become a brush salesman; but after a while he had realised that he wanted something more interesting to sell, and joined us instead. John was a wonderfully cheerful and optimistic man, and I trusted him enough to authorise payment of commission on deals for which he had no paperwork. "The paperwork won't be signed until next month", he would tell me; "but it's in the bag!" And surprisingly it always was.

I will tell you just two more of my Photoscan stories. The first, in the summer of 1969, involves me introducing our services to the senior management of Lewis's at a meeting in their Glasgow department store. They wanted me at such short notice that there was no time to book a sleeper, and Dorothy put me on the overnight train at Crewe with an ordinary second-class ticket. The train was not overcrowded, and I was beginning to look forward to a peaceful journey when at the very last minute I was joined in my compartment by a diminutive couple of somewhat doggy appearance. Between them they were carrying four modest baskets, each of which held two Mexican Chihuahuas. I learned that the next day would be the day of the annual dog show at Glasgow's Kelvin Hall.

At first it all seemed quite interesting. But throughout the night, the Chihuahuas were let out in rotation. The ones who were out yapped with excitement. The ones who remained in the baskets yapped in protest at not being out. I thought of making a protest myself, but just then one of the Chihuahuas gave me a nasty sort of growl, and I decided to keep quiet. Sleep was impossible. It was an unbelievably awful night. When the journey was almost over I washed and shaved in the toilet and did my best to freshen up, but when we pulled into Glasgow station at eight o'clock in the morning I felt far from my usual sunny self.

Breakfast cheered me up a little; but when I arrived at Lewis's soon after nine o'clock I knew that I would have to be efficient, knowledgeable and business-like if I was to have any chance of convincing these canny Scots that our equipment would save them money. After such a bad night, what hope did I have?

However, they seemed quite happy to spend their time talking about almost anything under the sun except the service which I had come to sell them. This was disconcerting. I knew that it wasn't just the Glasgow store that was at stake. It had been made clear to me that, if I could convince them of Photoscan's merits, we could expect orders for their stores in Birmingham, Manchester and London.

I kept trying to pull them back to the business in hand, with very little success. After a while we had coffee and made a general tour of the store. By the time we had finished the tour it was nearly twelve o'clock, and one of them looked at his watch and commented on the time and added: "Why don't we go across the road for a little refreshment?" It seemed early for lunch, but they all looked at their own watches and agreed with their colleague that it was an excellent moment for 'a little refreshment'.

'A little refreshment' turned out to mean a steady stream of large whiskies in a nearby bar where they were evidently much at home. I reckoned that I had no hope of matching them whisky for whisky and staying on my feet long enough to secure an order, so at the risk of being branded an impossible Sassenach I chose lager and stuck to it. This enabled me to keep the initiative; but I didn't dare throw my advantage away by disappearing to the gents, so as the hours went by and our liquid lunch continued, my distress in that department became extreme.

At last it was three o'clock and the bar closed, and in some mysterious way I had evidently satisfied them. For after we had gone back to their offices, it was less than half-an-hour before I had my order, and a formal authorization to survey all four stores for a major installation of Photoscan. I caught the train home and dined in the restaurant car a happy man.

Incidentally, when I returned to Scotland by car in connection with the installation, the police pulled me over for speeding, telling me that I had been driving at 95 mph. Subsequently I produced evidence that the car, according to its manufacturers, was only capable of doing 91 mph, and suggested that in those circumstances the case could only fairly be judged 'non proven'. Unfortunately the Scottish magistrate did not share my opinion, and fined me £15.

My final Photoscan story is about another much smaller installation in Glasgow, where the Scottish and Newcastle Brewery had a very small bar in one of the roughest districts. It was a very profitable place, simply because it sold a great deal of liquor. However there had been five managers in only two years.

The problem was that the managers and their families were threatened with violence if the more extreme elements did not get free liquor. It was not necessarily whisky or beer that was required. Indeed, one of the most popular brews was cheap red wine, which the customer would then lace heavily with neat methylated spirit.

We installed a Photoscan unit on the ceiling, enclosed in a metal cage so that it would be difficult for even the most resourceful customers to steal or destroy. The fact that the unit was so clearly visible also meant that those customers would be constantly reminded that if they misbehaved themselves, the manager could produce photographs which might be used as evidence; and so that he would never be out of reach of a switch, we put activator switches all round the premises.

The installation itself was a slightly unnerving experience for the engineers involved. The rumour had gone around that the installation was to be done, and they had to be locked in the premises all night and then whisked away by taxi first thing the following morning, as there was a real risk to their personal safety.

CHAPTER EIGHT

While we were building Photoscan, our other enterprises did not come to standstill, and nor did our developing family. The children's bed-times were fixed according to their ages, and this caused bad feeling if the current bed-time for an individual child meant that he or she was deprived of all or part of a particularly attractive television programme. The most popular serial was undoubtedly *Doctor Who*, though I remember Philip finding some of the characters so frightening that he watched the programme peering out from his hiding-place behind the settee, so that he could retreat into safety when any especially terrifying monster appeared.

John as the youngest boy preceded his brothers upstairs to bed, and got into the habit of leaning over the banisters for a last glimpse of the downstairs world he was being compelled to leave. On one occasion which is seared into my memory he leaned too far, and began a seemingly endless fall, which was broken at last by the Grand Piano. The Piano sustained only minor bruising; but Jonathan lost a great deal of blood and carries the scars of that encounter with him to this day. Dorothy rushed him to the out-patients' department of the Royal Salop Infirmary, where (thanks mainly to John's escapades) we would become comparatively well-known over the years. There was another particularly notable occasion a few years after this when he managed to pogo-stick right through a window, with dire consequences.

As for our other enterprises: during the late sixties we seemed to be taking on more and more. In retrospect, it was probably too much.

For one thing, we expanded our property interests. It happened like this. A group of Ministry properties near Market Drayton came up for auction and we decided that Longford Camp at Rosehill, on which the Ministry of Defence had just lavished £84,0000, would provide us with an outstanding opportunity to create an inland leisure centre.

Located around a ring road there were thirty buildings which could easily be converted into sixty brick-built self-contained chalets. There were also three main blocks of building, which had been the Sergeants' Mess, the Dining Hall complex and the NAAFI stores; and everything was contained in an attractive, level seventeen-acre site with good roads, mains water, drainage and electricity.

As if this were not enough, within a few months two adjoining fields became available, and I was able to acquire these and virtually double the amount of ground available at a modest cost. I felt almost overwhelming confidence that I was on to a financial winner. Not only were all the services in place, but there was ready access to the heart of England. With places like Birmingham and Wolverhampton only 30 to 45 miles away, I could create an ideal weekend resort for those Midlanders who might well be deterred by the prospect of a 200-mile round-trip to the coast.

Plan were drawn up and submitted to the Shropshire County Council, but to our amazement they were refused. I think the problem was that we were ten or fifteen years ahead of our time. In any case, there seemed to be good grounds for an appeal.

For one thing, the SCC had argued that the access from the site to the road was inadequate, with visibility being dangerously poor. We were able to prove that this was nonsense: the road was dead straight, and the visibility was a good 400 yards. For another, they described it as an undesirable activity in a rural area — but as our planning counsel said on our behalf, you could hardly have a holiday camp of this kind in the suburbs! However the appeal was turned down, and after a great deal of time and expense we appeared to have reached a dead-end.

I decided that the best available tactic was to put the ball back in the SCC's court, so I asked the Deputy Planning Officer what he expected us to do with the property. The DPO was close to retirement and seemed fairly indifferent. "Quite honestly", he said, "I'd like to see all these ex-Ministry properties bulldozed to the ground, and the land returned to what it was, farming land."

"If you work on that basis", I said rather cheekily, "you'd better start turning all agricultural land back into indigenous forest, because that's what it was before it was farming land."

Suddenly he seemed to come to life.

"All right then", he said briskly. "You've had some experience with industrial development. Why don't you put in an application for industrial use?"

I took his advice. However the then Labour Government's policy was to direct industry and new jobs into areas which they had selected; and so I needed to obtain industrial development certificates. This theoretically involved a complicated procedure. First I had to advertise for prospective tenants; then I was supposed to apply for industrial development certificates for their individual use; and only after that could I begin the lengthy business of applying for and obtaining planning consent.

In practice, with the connivance of several excellent prospective tenants, we made the units they required usable by providing the necessary facilities, smartened up the buildings and allowed them to move in. We then obtained the industrial development certificates and planning consent retrospectively. By this means we established seven or eight tenants comparatively quickly, something which would have been impossible if we had strictly observed the rules.

In the meantime the Condover Industrial Estate had been doing well; but Lynn Dewing's practical involvement was now minimal. Having inherited his farm, he had never had to learn the value of capital, and when we visited him once I was astonished to hear him say that he had spent £17,000 merely on renovating and decorating his dining-room. Spending such a sum for that purpose would have been unthinkable to us. My aim was always to plough money back into our companies so as to build them up. But when Lynn visited us, his only interest lay in asking: "What about a draw, Bob? Don't you think we might have a pull out of the firm?"

In 1969 we bought at auction on behalf of Lynn Dewing Ltd. a further Ministry of Defence property at Bomere Heath just outside Shrewsbury. This became the Leaton Industrial Estate; and its purchase led to our being approached by Simon Hillmale. He persuaded us to give him the financial backing to form a new company, Decor Manufacturing Ltd, which became one of our first tenants at Leaton.

Unfortunately Simon was a mercurial character who did not stick at anything for long; and the upshot was that he disappeared to New Zealand with £3,000 of our money — at least £30,000 in today's terms. Our solicitor John Yates advised us to write this off to experience. However we weren't in the habit of throwing away such large sums of money, and fortunately Simon Hillmale's distinctive name made him comparatively easy to trace. Using attorneys in New Zealand we were then able to have a charge placed on a house he had bought; and when Simon decided to part from his wife and sell the house, he could not get his hands on his share of the proceeds until our charge had been settled. So we received our £3,000 plus costs.

This was all very satisfactory, but did not solve the main problem which was that Decor Manufacturing Ltd. had no manager. Eventually we appointed Barry Swann, a very personable, erudite, self-confident gentleman who came highly recommended, though it was not long before we were forced to accept that he was one of our failures. When we had first met him, incidentally, we had taken him out to dinner, and allowed him to choose the wine. Perhaps the manner in which he did this should have put us on our guard. He tasted the first bottle, turned up his nose, and politely suggested to the wine waiter that it was fit only for the next day's sherry trifle.

Another small company we backed at the same time was Decorhire. This was the brainchild of John Weston-Edwards and Peter Blower, and their plan was to hire prints of classic pictures to schools, hotels, public houses, clubs and so on. At first they were very successful at placing these prints; but after a while they grew bored and we found ourselves with yet another business on our hands.

1969 was also the year when we decided that we could not go on indefinitely trying to run all our various businesses from Pimley Manor, where the necessary offices had grown to fill the whole of the mews. Then onto the market came St. Chad's Vicarage, an eighteenth-century building complete with an archaic basement kitchen from which a dumb waiter carried the food up to the vicar's dining-room. Our pre-auction offer of £10,000 was turned down. This seemed disappointing at the time, but actually saved us £1,000; because we were able to buy it at auction for only £9,000. The conversion from traditional vicarage to modern offices and stores involved a great deal of work for our growing building division, at that time being managed by Ken Williams, who had come to us from the house-builders Ashley, Ashley and Newbrook.

We decided to call the converted building Claremont House. It was opened in 1970 by John Langford-Holt, the Conservative Member of Parliament for Shrewsbury; and among the host of VIPs was Mrs Dyer, the Mayor of Shrewsbury, to whom four-year-old Janet presented a bouquet. Claremont House provided us with office facilities for twelve companies including A.J. Manson Ltd., Lynn Dewing Ltd., Rosehill (Market Drayton) Ltd., Photoscan (Central) Ltd., Decor Manufacturing Ltd, R. J. & D. E. Freeman, and Q-Hire; and we had soon begun the process of gathering all our companies into a single entity to be known as the Claremont Group. At the same time we hired perky, ebullient little Jack Jones as our first Company Secretary.

We had also decided to use Claremont House to demonstrate the most up-to-date surveillance facilities that we could offer through Photoscan, and so we had installed a comprehensive closed-circuit TV system. It included an advanced pan, tilt and zoom installation on the roof; and numerous cameras and monitors inside the building. There was also a console on the desk in my office, which enabled me to see and talk to people in different parts of Claremont House at the touch of a button.

However, 1970 turned out to be a very stressful year.

For one thing my workload was increasing significantly. I would do a morning's

THE CLAREMONT GROUP

A. J. MANSON LTD.
" Q " HIRE LTD.
R. J. & D. E. FREEMAN
LYNN DEWING (Properties) LTD.
PHOTO-SCAN (Central) LTD.
ROSEHILL (Market Drayton) LTD.
" TRAVELON "
PHOTO-SCAN (South Wales) LTD.
CORAL POOLS LTD.
DECORPRINTS
DECORHIRE LTD.
NEWMAN ASSOCIATES

We have 'Gone to Town'...

...on our New Premises, which are of Historic interest, situated in a prominent part of Shrewsbury
Our new address is now:
CLAREMONT HOUSE
CLAREMONT BANK
SHREWSBURY

SHREWSBURY
(STD.0743)
57341 2 3 4

Twelve companies move into Claremont House

work in my office at Claremont House, followed by an afternoon at the Decor Manufacturing Offices over at the industrial estate at Leaton; and then I would take work home to my study at Pimley Manor for dictation. On top of this I always found it necessary to spend a couple of hours on a Sunday night preparing for the coming week. My monthly journey to London for a Photoscan meeting came as something of a relief. I would breakfast on the train going down, and have dinner in the train coming back up. Being on my own I nearly always found myself sharing a table for two, and I made a point of getting into conversation. This was intensely rewarding. Even when people appeared to be most unpromising, and it was very difficult to break the ice, they would eventually turn out to be most interesting companions.

For another thing, there was a good deal of friction between the various companies sharing Claremont House. It had been agreed by all parties that the costs of running the building should be shared out according to certain fixed percentages. Nor was this agreement surprising since A.J. Manson Ltd. and Photoscan Central Ltd., the two companies which were wholly controlled by me, had each been allocated 35%. This meant that I was personally responsible for 70% of the costs; and yet some members who were responsible for only 5% of the costs proved extremely difficult when asked to pay their dues. Still more annoying, tenants on the Leaton Industrial Estate who were enjoying a preferential rate of only half-a-crown per square foot per annum had the gall to say that they only wanted to rent their space, not buy it. Most difficult of all, we were severely undercapitalised: hardly surprising, since all the capital input had come from ourselves.

There were also complications involving Lynn Dewing. Not long after we had acquired Leaton Estates we had become aware that Lynn was bouncing cheques. There were anxious telephone calls from people asking whether we had seen him? They wanted to get in touch with him, either because of one of those bouncing cheques, or because he had a painting of theirs which he had neither paid for nor returned.

Eventually Lynn approached us and asked whether we would buy him out. He had some grand scheme which would put everything right. He was always having grand schemes: at one stage I think he had set his heart on obtaining the Royal Warrant for supplying the Queen's stables with fodder, but I doubt whether it came to anything.

At any rate, we bought him out for some £22,000. Fortunately our bank was delighted to help us out, but this stretched our resources to the limit, and placed me under more stress than ever.

We were also involved in yet more new businesses.

I mentioned that Ken Williams had come to us from Ashley Ashley and Newbrook. I didn't add that he had fallen out with Gordon Ashley, a one-time friend of ours with whom we too had had severe problems. However, Williams himself turned out to be a difficult man, and we were not sorry when he approached us saying that he would resign as building manager, if we would back a new company to be known as Coral Pools Ltd. which was being set up by him and Pete Newbrook, who had also become disenchanted with Gordon Ashley, despite the fact that he was Gordon's brother-in-law.

I realised that I was already overworked, but it was put to me that Ken Williams and Pete Newbrook and their associate Bates Critchlow, a swimming-pool engineer, would

Alma House, one of the properties turned into flats by Ken Williams for Newman Associates

be doing all the work. My task would only be to put up some money and provide them with premises. So Coral Pools was established.

At the same time Williams and Newbrook had lined up a project which involved turning two houses into flats. Once again they wanted me to back them on a fifty-fifty basis, with Ken Williams arranging for the work to be done; and this venture was set up as a partnership under the name of Newman Associates.

Unfortunately there was a fundamental weakness in these arrangements. Completely unknown to us, Pete Newbrook was an alcoholic, with bottles of whiskey stored in every conceivable place, including toilet cisterns. When sober he was a delightful man; but he could not cope with the pressures of life and, to cut a long story short, he drove off into the Welsh hills in his Mercedes and took his own life. Gordon Ashley appears to have blamed Ken Williams for his brother-in-law's suicide, and the story circulated round Shrewsbury that he told Ken to leave town. Whatever the truth of that, Ken Williams left our organisation and moved at very short notice to Prestatyn.

Pete Newbrook's suicide and Ken Williams's departure increased the pressures on me considerably.

First, I was left in control of the nine flats belonging to Newman Associates. After some difficult negotiations with the solicitors to Pete Newbrook's executors, we bought out their 50% for £16,000. [In the long term, this turned out to be a sound investment. In recent years we have been renovating and selling the flats as they fall vacant. We still have two in hand, and the seven that we have sold have realised in total well over £200,000.]

Second, I was left in charge of Coral Pools Ltd., a company building swimming-pools with a number of outstanding commitments. The result was that in a very short time I had to learn a great deal about building swimming-pools, and my level of overwork, already much too high, rose into the stratosphere.

By June 1971 I had at last managed to solve the cash problems which had been dogging me; but one day that month I was out at the Leaton offices when I felt so ill that I had to telephone Dorothy and ask her to come and fetch me, which she did. Not long afterwards I was diagnosed as suffering from a nervous breakdown. My doctor said that he could give me some medication that would keep me going for a short while, but he would prefer not to do this unless it was absolutely necessary.

So Dorothy stepped into the breach, just as she had done six years before when I had been suffering from pneumonia. She took complete control of all our businesses, and for six months I did no work at all. Curiously I have virtually no recollection of those six months. I had over-stretched myself so severely that it would take me a long time to get back into my stride. For months I could not face meeting anyone or speaking to anyone on the telephone. In fact my antipathy towards the telephone has lasted to this day.

CHAPTER NINE

Having vastly over-reached myself, I had ended by placing a massive and unreasonable burden upon my wife Dorothy. So as soon as I was once again capable of work we began a gradual rationalisation of our activities.

Photoscan was the first to go. Fortunately Photoscan London were just as keen to buy our Midland franchises as we were to sell them, and they then took over most of our staff and vacated our premises. John Hanrahan, incidentally, went on to found his own surveillance company; and although it was on a much smaller scale than Photoscan it seemed to provide him with everything he wanted in life, including ample time and opportunity to go fishing.

Selling Photoscan was a blow to me, because I could see the vast potential both for security services and for closed-circuit television. It was a decision made simpler by memories of our traumatic visit to Los Angeles, where it had been easy to see that it was never likely to become the world-wide force of which we had envisaged becoming a part. And in fact we were lucky to get out when we did. Our whole service was based on fixed-price three-year leases, including on-site maintenance; and when during the next few years inflation went through the roof, Photoscan London were so badly hit that they had to sell a controlling interest in their company.

ERB Ltd and Coral Pools Ltd., we closed down as fast as we reasonably could, but not before I had learned enough about building swimming-pools to be confident about building our own, which I did at Pimley Manor in 1972. This has not only provided the Manor with an attractive amenity, but has also been a very considerable benefit to my health.

Decor Manufacturing and Decorhire were both moved back to our offices at Pimley, their administration being merged with A.J. Manson Ltd. We gradually wound down Decor Manufacturing; but we persevered for a few years with Decorhire, changing its name to Western Picture Library. We felt that there was a worthwhile business to be developed, and Janet Edwards, ably supported by Bridget Trow, did good work in this sphere, developing a side-line in mail-order prints and pre-manufactured self-assembly picture frames. However Dorothy and I could not give Western Picture Library the attention it needed to build it up into anything worthwhile, and eventually we wound it down.

In the meantime there had been a thoroughly unprofitable spin-off, in the form of Encapsulation and Resin Bonding Ltd., a company run by a Mr. Walsh and actively sponsored and encouraged by our old Photoscan employee Mike Maddox. The point was that Mr. Walsh hoped to produce in plastic moulds a type of heavily-patterned gold-finished picture framing which Western Picture Library used a great deal, and which was very expensive because much of it came all the way from Czechoslovakia. Mr. Walsh produced prototype after prototype after prototype, while he occupied our premises and was given a great deal of support; but sadly he never actually managed to get into production, and all his well-meaning efforts ended in failure.

As for our Q-Hire business: we had been having serious doubts about the future of self-drive commercial vehicle hire. The amount of work involved and capital employed was increasing much faster than the net profits. All our hiring had been based on allowing the customer unlimited mileage, chiefly because we knew how vulnerable speedometers were to fiddling. All that a hirer had to do was to reach under the dashboard and disconnect the speedo cable, and no mileage at all would be registered! But with the development of the motorway system, average mileages were increasing dramatically. All it took was for someone to travel far away, while neglecting a broken or slipping fan belt, and we could be faced with a breakdown involving huge travel costs, and a vehicle with at best a completely flat battery, and at worst an over-heated and irreparably damaged engine. So over a couple of years we gradually phased out this operation.

At the same time, we decided to extend our interests as travel agents; and to reflect this change of direction we altered the name of Q-Hire to Travelon (Midlands) Ltd; and then in 1972 we opened a branch at 12 Shoplatch in the centre of Shrewsbury, run by Jack Myddle while Kate remained in charge of our original Travel Agents in Crewe. Almost immediately the Shrewsbury branch produced double the turnover of the Crewe branch; and our arrangement with the Myddles (who had now moved out of the company flat in Crewe and bought their own house in Audlem) worked very successfully until 1976.

A further rationalisation involved combining Newman Associates with RJ and DE Freeman, while the building work was continued by AJ Manson Ltd. Finally we restructured the management of our industrial estates. Up to this point they had been operating as two separate companies, with Condover and Leaton Industrial Estates being part of Lynn Dewing Properties Ltd., while Rosehill Industrial Estate was owned by Rosehill Market Drayton Ltd.

In the mid-1970s we merged Lynn Dewing Ltd. with Rosehill Market Drayton Ltd., and the whole enterprise was merged under the name Shropshire Industrial Estates. Extending and renovating old buildings, and building new ones, this company went from strength to strength, increasing turnover and profitability by at least 10% per annum for more than twenty years. As for Lynn Dewing: I'm afraid to say that his marriage broke up, and I believe he served a term of imprisonment for fraud: a sad end to what should have been a success story for him as well as for us.

Our reorganisation complete, the period until 1979 was one of comparative calm with regular holidays and only a moderate amount of stress. One factor in this calm was the presence of Betty Rigby, who had arrived in July 1972 to take over accounts from our elderly part-timer Fred Bennett. Betty would stay with us for eighteen years; and for much of that time she managed to be completely efficient while utterly resisting the allure of modern technology. Soon after she first came I bought her an electronic calculator, but she took one look at it and said: "I don't want that thing in here! When the day comes that I can't add up a column of figures, that will be the end."

However there were occasional alarms.

In 1974, for example, I began running into serious problems with the Rosehill Estate. The point was that when I was dealing with the first planning consents, the Deputy Planning Officer of the time had asked me to come in and see him. He had then explained that the Planners were worried by the possibility that at some stage in the future we might sell individual buildings to different owners. Under those circumstances, it could be difficult for them to maintain adequate planning control.

'Before' and 'After' photos of part of the Rosehill Industrial Estate

So would we accept limited fifteen-year planning consents? Since I had no intention of selling any part of this developing asset, I had readily agreed; and from then on we had regularly obtained planning consents as and when required on a fifteen-year basis.

In 1974, however, planning responsibility was devolved from the Shropshire County Council to the local district councils. I was concerned that there might be a change of policy, but was assured by Mr. Revell, the new Planning Officer, that this would not be so. There were then five of our applications in the pipeline. Two were dealt with by the SCC and passed; but the other three, which had not been approved by the change-over date of 1 April 1974, were transferred to the North Shropshire District Council and promptly refused.

This was the start of a prolonged nightmare. My letters to the NSDC went unanswered, and twice I turned up for appointments with named officers only to find them mysteriously absent. In the end I was left with only two options. One was to allow the estate to die on its feet, something which I found unthinkable. The other was to ignore the planners completely. This would set me on a collision course with the NSDC, but what else was I to do? I proceeded to implement substantial lettings, to carry out extensive renovation work, and even to extend some of the existing buildings. All the time I was ploughing back the rental income into the estate, with the aim of improving its quality and adding to the rent roll.

Another difficulty: I mentioned that our Travelon arrangements with Kate and Jack Myddle worked very successfully until 1976. That was the year when the four of us: Kate, Jack, Dorothy and I; went together to the ABTA conference in Miami, and

The Shrewsbury branch of Travelon at 25 Shoplatch

stayed together afterwards for a post-conference holiday. It was therefore an unpleasant shock on the day we returned from America to be told quite calmly by the Myddles that they proposed to buy out our interest in the two branches of Travelon for the derisory sum of only £5,000. If we did not accept, they told us, they would be gone within a couple of months.

We had no option but to terminate their employment forthwith, and change the locks on both premises. This naturally created considerable problems. Dorothy took over overall management of Travelon, and also handled the day-to-day management of the Shrewsbury branch. At the same time we began advertising for managers.

Soon we had appointed Vic Green to the Crewe branch. Vic was honest and well-meaning, but unfortunately keeping proper records was not his strong point, and he created much agony and anguish in Shrewsbury, where the book-keeping was done. It was not so much the mistakes he made, as his efforts to correct those mistakes, which had our book-keeper, Betty Rigby, practically tearing her hair out with frustration. However in due course we were able to sell the lease and goodwill of the Crewe branch to a Mr. Lancaster for £20,000. The only fly in this particular ointment was that we succumbed to the temptation of accepting £5,000 of the purchase price in cash, a weakness which subsequently involved us in all the horrors of a thorough-going tax inquiry.

As for the overall management of Travelon (Midlands) Ltd, and the running of the Shrewsbury branch: we felt that we had found the perfect solution in the appointment of Dorothy Munnerley, an experienced travel agent from Liverpool. However, we had hardly installed her and fixed her up with a furnished flat when her mother in Liverpool was taken seriously ill, and Dorothy had to leave us at a moment's notice. This put us back to square one.

We then obtained the services of Malcolm Soutar. His qualifications were beyond reproach: a married man with a charming wife and two little girls, he had over twenty years' experience in the travel industry; and he would work for us for many years. Unfortunately however Malcolm's appointment was a major tactical error, largely because of his strongly-held left-wing views.

Let me explain. The fact that Malcolm Soutar became a Labour Councillor soon after coming to Shrewsbury was of no significance to us one way or the other. We have never asked any of our prospective employees to declare either their religious or their political affiliations, believing it to be none of our business. Unfortunately Malcolm's socialism was so extreme that he gave the impression of being violently biassed against anyone whom he saw as a capitalist. In practical terms, this meant anyone who had any money.

Now obviously in the travel industry a great deal of the bread-and-butter of the business comes from arranging package holidays to places like Malta and Majorca, ferry crossings to Ireland or to the Continent, theatre tickets for a night out in London, and so on and so forth. But the cream comes from cruises, round-the-world holidays, and world-wide travel to places like South Africa or Australia. Unfortunately, anyone who could afford the cream was an abomination to Malcolm Soutar. I am sure he did not realise it, but he came across to wealthy customers as being so rude that he could hardly bear even to pass the time of day with them. The result was that the best business (including some of our personal friends) went elsewhere. As if this were not enough, he became so unpopular with the rest of the staff that we were faced with a choice between letting them go, or letting him go. You may imagine which option we chose.

The next incumbent was Ron Morgan, an enthusiastic and successful salesman who built the business up substantially in the new premises to which we had moved in the centre of Shrewsbury. But then news came that Ron's American father-in-law was dying of cancer. Ron and his wife immediately went to see him on an extended holiday; and the next thing we heard was that Ron had found a job working for a travel agent in South Carolina, and was not coming back.

Subsequently Ron Morgan did in fact return: but not to manage Travelon. Instead, much to our disappointment, he opened another travel agency in Shrewsbury in direct opposition to our own business, which was now being managed by Sue Owen. Sue had been with us since leaving school, and knew the business extremely well. Unfortunately she could not stay with us for long; but during her time as Manageress, Travelon would make its biggest ever annual profit.

CHAPTER TEN

The management of furnished flats occupied a great deal of our time for some twenty-five years, from 1964 (when we began at Pimley) until 1988/89 when we began disposing of the forty flats under our control. During that time we had some four hundred tenants; and I must say at once that by far the majority of them were sensible, reasonable people. Sadly however, it is nearly always more entertaining reading about the difficult people than the easy ones, and I have a few stories which may amuse you.

Of course when we began, we had only common sense to guide us. We furnished our flats extremely fully; and since many of our early lettings were to army personnel, we arranged the most detailed inventory check with incoming and outgoing tenants, counting everything down to the last teaspoon and even making sure that the toilet cistern was flushing properly. However as we began dealing more and more with civilians, we began finding that these exercises were taking up too much of our time, and so we simply inserted a clause into each new tenancy agreement putting the onus on the tenant to inform us about any items that were missing or broken.

Now, about the people. I remember one of our early tenants at Pimley who had obviously fallen on hard times, but insisted on telling everyone that his address was Pimley Manor, with the result that all his post was delivered to us and not to his flat. Then there was the Admiral's daughter who appointed herself unofficial guardian of one of our larger properties. Her self-imposed 'duties' included keeping a close watch over the moral behaviour of the younger tenants in the house; and frequently she jumped to conclusions which were totally incorrect.

We began with a 'no pets' rule; and I am sorry to say that whenever we made an exception to this rule (which we did occasionally in the early days) we lived to regret it. It was difficult not to sympathise with the owner of the old pet dog who 'isn't a nuisance to anybody' — and yet when he left, his dog had damaged every door in the flat. It was difficult not to allow a sweet old lady to keep an old pussy-cat who 'hasn't got long to live' — and yet when she left, we had to replace the carpet.

Parties occasionally caused trouble, usually in flats occupied by girls who couldn't control gate-crashers. In fact the worst tenants we ever had were three girls living together, and we made a rule against it. Boys swarmed round them like bees around a honey-pot, and their parties would overflow into the halls and landings and upset the other tenants.

When a real problem blew up at night, I sometimes had to go down with our German Shepherd dog held on a close rein. She was really as soft as anything, and would never have bitten anyone, but she usually frightened people enough to make them toe the line.

More than once we had problems with drug addicts; but with my Photoscan experience I was able to provide the police with surveillance facilities so that they could deal with matters before they got completely out of hand. There was one particular occasion when two girls took over a newly decorated flat up at Pimley Manor and immediately painted it throughout in psychedelic colours. Before long they had also acquired a most terrible reputation; and when I had gathered enough evidence of their activities I changed the locks and turned them away. They immediately contacted the local Council and complained that I had no right to exclude them from their flat; and one of the Council officials actually tried to tell me that I had committed a criminal offence. I countered this by stating that I would undoubtedly have been condoning criminal offences had I allowed their tenancy to continue; and when the chips were down they were not inclined to make an issue of the matter.

Other excitements over the years have included more than one attempted murder. In one case a man was breaking down a flat door with a machete in an attempt to get at his girl-friend. Another man was convicted of murder, but not on our premises, and he was not actually convicted until after he had left us.

On another occasion we woke to a wife who was banging on our door after midnight, and screaming out: "Help! Help!" Apparently her husband hadn't taken the tablets on which he depended if he was to remain in a reasonable frame of mind. We called the police and they came along with a doctor who happened to be our doctor, and who was thumped in the face for his pains.

On another occasion Dorothy suddenly became aware that there was an intruder in one of our unoccupied bedrooms in Pimley Manor and she called the police, who arrived very promptly. However, it turned out the intruder was not a burglar at all. In fact he was the son of a local QC. He had intended paying a midnight call upon a girl living in one of our first-floor flats, and had mistakenly come in through the wrong window. The police recognised him at once; and perhaps it was his father's influence which saved him from being charged with breaking and entering.

Several tenants left with various of our furnishings. The curtains went most often, especially when a young couple were about to set up home on their own for the first time; but we had one tenant, who had come to us highly recommended, who went off with all the carpets.

As for non-payment of rent: we must have heard every excuse in the book. If they were clever enough they could get three or even four months in arrears, and of course a handful of the hard-luck stories were genuine. Sometimes we received cheques which bounced; but the most common event was to be told of a cheque that was 'in the post' but which never actually arrived.

In later years it became common for Social Services to pay the rent for tenants of ours who were unemployed. The difficulty was that when the tenants found work, it was tempting for them to continue to allow their rent to be paid. They were always discovered in the end; but then, most unfairly, it was our legal responsibility to repay the excess rent, and not theirs. This was the biggest single factor in our decision to begin selling off the flats as the opportunity arose.

One of the more daunting calls I had to make was to a flat where it was clear that our tenants were flagellation addicts. I found the woman particularly unattractive, not to say actually threatening, and having to stand close to her in a flat whose walls were covered with whips, straps and other instruments of human torture was most unnerving.

Another unusual tenant was a nice little man who lived in a ground-floor flat. There seemed to be a lady around at times, but we never saw them together. Then, having been with us for some considerable time, he simply disappeared. We were aware of this fairly quickly, because he had several employees who visited the flat regularly to take instructions from him, and they told us that, as they put it, he had 'done a bunk'. What had actually happened we shall never know; but I suspect something odd, because when we investigated the flat we found that he appeared to have left all his personal belongings behind. But what was most strange was a significant wardrobe of vaguely familiar ladies' clothes, a collection of ladies' shoes, and some sort of certificate declaring that he was a registered transvestite. So he and his 'lady-friend' had in fact been one and the same. No wonder we had never seen them out together!

Another tenant was always immaculately turned out, but her flat was always absolutely filthy. At one point I had it completely redecorated: not easy, because the decorators almost went on strike in protest at working in such dirty conditions. I then took her to task on the subject; but when she said to me: "Mr. Freeman, I am allergic to dirt, so I can't clean: it upsets me too much", I must admit that I was at a loss for an answer.

By contrast, the cleanest tenant we ever had was a young Muslim, whose flat was so spotless that it would have been perfectly safe to eat a meal off the floor. An extraordinary character, who spun the most wonderful tales about why his rent was late, he went from one job to another. At one stage he was a mundane clerk working at British Telecom; at another (appropriately perhaps for a keep-fit fanatic) he had become a kick-dance performer and founded a kick-dancing club; at another he was a Financial Consultant: presumably a high-flying one, because he turned up first in a grey and then in a red Porsche. Not that he could drive: but by then he had attracted a girlfriend who drove for him. At one stage he disappeared for an extended period, and then turned up in a taxi saying that he would be back in a few minutes with all the rent he owed us. In fact he must have come to say good-bye, because we never saw him again; and eventually we had to dispose of the considerable effects he had left in the flat to defray his outstanding rent. I sometimes wonder what happened to him.

We also had our share of tragedy. One tenant died in a head-on car crash; and we nearly lost another one who was helping to build the Ironbridge Power Station and fell some 40 feet from the scaffolding. Our saddest loss was that of a perfect gentleman who had lived in our smallest flat for nearly ten years. He talked very little, but when he did he sometimes mentioned a nephew, whom he hoped would return from Australia and start farming with him. But the nephew never did come and one day our gentleman went down by the river with his 12-bore shotgun and shot himself. I understand that he had an appointment to see his doctor that week and was convinced that he had cancer. After his suicide, a brother about whom we knew nothing, and who evidently hadn't seen him for years, came up from the south of England to collect his belongings.

CHAPTER ELEVEN

As in all families, schools were a major factor in our life for a long time: in our case, with four children, the fifteen years from 1965 to 1980. Nature doesn't always arrange things very sensibly, and I sometimes think how annoying it is that these days, when I have no pressing need to get up early in the morning, I cannot sleep for more than five or six hours at a time. Yet during the entire period when I had to do the 'school-run' each morning, it took two alarm clocks to wake me at seven so that I could get the children into the car by eight-fifteen.

It all began in a comparatively low key with the children going to 'The Rocks' nursery school. This was presided over by Mrs. Bird, with her husband Mr. Bird ('the lesser Bird' as I thought of him) somewhere in the background.

Then the boys went on to Kingsland Grange: an impressive name for a school, and an impressive central building impressively presided over by the Brothers Groves; but the actual classrooms in those days were what seemed to be a fairly ramshackle bunch of miscellaneous temporary buildings. The highlight of the school year was the combined school sports and prize-giving day, when we parents earned our tea and buns by indulging in three-legged and wheel-barrow races, at the end of which the venerable Mr. Groves senior would sometimes appear and dispense prizes to the more deserving cases.

On to Shrewsbury School. We had put Christopher's name down for Shrewsbury in

Me and Dorothy in 1978 with (standing between us from left to right) Christopher, Janet, John and Philip.

1961 when he was only a few months old, after the then headmaster Mr. Petersen had taken us on a conducted tour. Even at that time, when the fees were around £600 per annum, we wondered how on earth we would be able to afford them out of taxed income. We could not have foreseen that by the time we had three sons at Shrewsbury School, the fees would have escalated to over £1,000 per boy per term just for day-boy accommodation.

By the time Christopher reached Shrewsbury School, Mr. Wright had taken over as Headmaster; and he himself would be shortly replaced by Mr. Anderson and his charming wife Poppy. I should add that we enjoyed a particularly happy relationship with the boys' Housemaster David Gee, a wise man who has become a life-long friend.

Christopher made a late decision to move on from Shrewsbury to Cirencester Agricultural College. Before he could be accepted, he had to spend a year working on a farm. He then obtained his diploma, but a spell on another farm convinced him that farming was not what he wanted to do for the rest of his life, and in a complete change of direction he joined the Cirencester Police Force.

Philip distinguished himself on the River Severn, rowing in the Shrewsbury Eights and earning many trophies culminating in one which he gained for rowing in the national under-16 Eights. He went on to study accountancy for two years at Nottingham Polytechnic, after which he entered a local firm of accountants. However it was not long before he joined the family firm telling me, to my considerable pleasure: "I would be foolish not to join the firm and build on the foundation which you have created."

In his early days, Jonathan showed considerable strength of character. Persisting in his view that he should not be wasting time on unimportant things like Latin, he preferred to spend his time in the craft workshop; and he seemed set for great things when in 1982, in partnership with another boy, he won the Young Engineer of Great Britain award and several other distinctions. He was readily accepted by Oxford Polytechnic and gained a diploma in building construction. Then, after a short spell with the house builders Second City, he too joined the family firm.

I had hoped that with Phil and Jon both in the firm it would not be long before I was able to retire and leave my sons to take the firm forward to greater things. Indeed, I am sure that this would have happened but for John's marriage to Linda Came, who appeared to have little interest in being part of the greater Freeman family. She soon made it clear that in her view John could not be loyal both to the family firm and to his marriage, and he naturally chose his marriage. The subsequent difficulties meant that for two years the family was torn apart. Members of the family hardly spoke to each other in the office, and company meetings were particularly stressful, since John seemed reluctant to take any decision, however small, without referring back to his wife.

Inevitably this had a most damaging effect upon the company; and I was particularly upset when Dorothy began coming in for a good deal of criticism. Eventually the three Directors: I myself, Dorothy and Philip, decided that there was only one option; and I undertook one of the most distressing tasks of my life: that of telling John that someone was going to have to leave the firm, and it had been decided that it should be him. This decision was then followed by many months of expensive negotiations between our solicitors and John's solicitors before we were able to arrive at a financial settlement which was mutually agreeable.

As for Janet: she was happy at the Junior High School for girls under Miss Bligh, but decidedly unhappy at the Senior High. So we transferred her to Adcote, then under the governance of Mrs Chechet. Adcote, in its beautiful Norman Shaw mansion originally built for Rebecca Darby, was a happy school where Janet spent several rewarding years.

On leaving school Janet soon established an interest in nursing. She spent three happy years qualifying at Hereford, where (with help from us) she bought and renovated a house. This meant that she could supplement her income by taking in a series of carefully controlled male lodgers.

Subsequently she sold the house for a substantial profit and moved back to Shrewsbury, where she spent the next two years training to be a midwife. It was most unpleasant for her to find, on the very day that she qualified, that the Shrewsbury Hospital had no further requirement for midwives, so that she was immediately unemployed.

However Janet has great resilience and she successfully applied for the position of Sister at Bedstone College, where she was responsible for over two hundred boys and girls. A cottage (delightful once it had been renovated), a number of useful perks and much more money than she had ever earned before, helped to make this a very happy period in her life.

One of Janet's responsibilities at Bedstone was to take children to the dentist in Knighton. Now the dentist's wife was an outstandingly successful matchmaker. It was she who first introduced Janet to John Bowen, and the upshot was a fairy-tale wedding on 30 July 1994, with the reception being held in a marquee on the lawn of Pimley Manor.

CHAPTER TWELVE

Holidays and travel have been among the major rewards for a lifetime of hard work, though even holidays can be disastrous at time. In the early days of our marriage we used to visit my Mother occasionally in her Sussex cottage; but it had only two bedrooms and Dorothy always reckoned that you had to be pregnant to be given one of them. Otherwise there were a number of wooden sheds for which we had different names, such as 'the rabbit hutch'. Lesser mortals who weren't pregnant had to bring sleeping bags and make do with one of those.

It was in the summer of 1963 that Dorothy and I took our first holiday outside the UK, travelling to Benidorm in a Ford motor-home with our two sons (Chris was then two-and-a-half, and Philip just six months), our friends Roy and Olive Adlard, and our mother's help Ira Corfield. In addition to the motor-home we had a tent, which had been a bargain at only £2/10s/0d with six tokens from packets of Kellogg's Cornflakes. Roy and I slept in the tent, and all the others somehow managed to squeeze into the motor-home. On arriving in Benidorm we took possession of a gorgeous villa where, with an exchange rate of 235 pesetas to the pound, food and wine flowed in abundance.

The following year we travelled to Spain again, this time in a Bedford 12-seater, which we needed because Jonathan had been born, and we had taken another family of five with us: our friends Gordon and Eileen Ashley and their three children. Unfortunately this holiday was not a great success: indeed it almost ended in court. The journey down, which included an overnight stop at Rouen, was amicable enough. Certainly, we shouldered all the travelling expenses; but that was all right. It had been agreed that we should do so on the way down, with the Ashleys taking their turn on the way back.

However, once we had arrived in Calella (to the north-east of Barcelona), Gordon got it into his head that he wanted to have nothing to do with us. This naturally created some tension, though it didn't matter too much while we were actually in Spain, because fortunately we had booked separate apartments, one above the other. On the return journey, however, we were inevitably forced together, and feelings ran high because (apart from putting some petrol in the tank) Gordon completely reneged on his agreement to pay for the travelling expenses. This was very awkward for us because we had little money left; but it seemed impossible to reason with him. So we lived on a very restricted diet for a day or two; and (although the matter was finally settled out of court) on our return to Shropshire we realised that if we wanted any justice in the matter we had no alternative but to institute legal proceedings. A sad end to what should have been a wonderful holiday.

After this, our early family holidays were taken mainly in Ireland. Jim Manson had left us *Barnagearah* in his will; and so, not wanting two Irish cottages, and preferring *Barnagearah*, we had sold *The Golden Gate*. Jim had only just begun restoring *Barnagearah*, but it was on a wonderful site; and gradually, with the help of grants from Cork County Council and the Irish Government, we had turned a one-up, one-down mud-floor Irish cottage into a delightful holiday home with three bedrooms, bathroom, living-room and kitchen. For short periods we had imported some building expertise from England, in the form of a carpenter and a plumber; and we also enjoyed the part-time service of an Irish labourer called Shaun. However we did most of the work ourselves, including the installation of a quarter of a mile of water mains, which brought the water under its own pressure to a collecting tank in the middle of a field; and the installation of an automatic electric pump which lifted the water the rest of the way up the hill to *Barnagearah*.

By the summer of 1965 *Barnagearah* was almost ready for occupation; and we travelled to Ireland with our recently-acquired Sprite 400 caravan. During the journey it was loaded down with building materials and kitchen appliances; and when we reached *Barnagearah* we camped in it until we had bedrooms fit for use.

For the next eleven years we were keen caravanners, going on adventurous family holidays to Wales, the West Country, Scotland, Ireland, France and Spain. In the summer of 1966, after Janet's birth, we realised that the Sprite 400 had become far too small. Managing bedtime for two adults, four children and a dog was like putting together a complicated jigsaw, with parents in a double-bed, Chris in a hammock, Philip and Jon end-to-end in a single bed, Sally the dog on the floor and Janet in a carry-cot. So we upgraded to the more spacious Sprite Major.

On our next visit to Spain, in 1968, we set out by car for Llafranch, where we were to share a large villa with Mike Maddox and his family. We spent several days on the road in our Peugeot 404, called 'Elsie' because the number plate read ELC 993. Elsie felt the strain of the long journey down, and when we arrived I had to do some repairs which involved removing the spark plugs. This involved me in a heart-stopping crisis when one of the spark plug terminals went down the plug-hole. With limited tools and extremely limited financial resources, the idea of having either to remove the cylinder head myself, or to pay someone else to do so, was almost unthinkable. However, after I had been fishing with pieces of wire for several hours, the gods decided to smile on me, and out through the plug-hole came the missing plug terminal.

One reason for our feeling comparatively poor was that the Spanish maid who came with the apartment had volunteered to produce a special celebratory meal for us all. We were given a list of the ingredients required; and the Paella she produced was certainly very enjoyable. Unfortunately it had also made a substantial hole in our holiday budget. Fortunately a reasonably good Spanish champagne was only 35 pesetas per bottle in those days. There was even a cheaper brew going for 25 pesetas per bottle, but we disdained that for the better variety: which helped to make the evenings extremely companionable.

The following year we travelled with the Maddoxes again, this time flying to Malta. This might have been a still more convivial holiday, because the bus to the hotel was only a quarter full, yet there was a 'courtesy' half-bottle of red wine on every seat, and our enterprising children gathered as many bottles as they could carry. Sadly, when we opened the first half-bottle at the hotel, we found that its contents were undrinkable.

Another disappointment was that the hotel to which we were bussed was not the one we had booked. In some ways this was just as well, because the one we had booked was only half-built. However the staff of the alternative hotel treated us like second-class citizens. This was particularly evident in the dining-room. Instead of

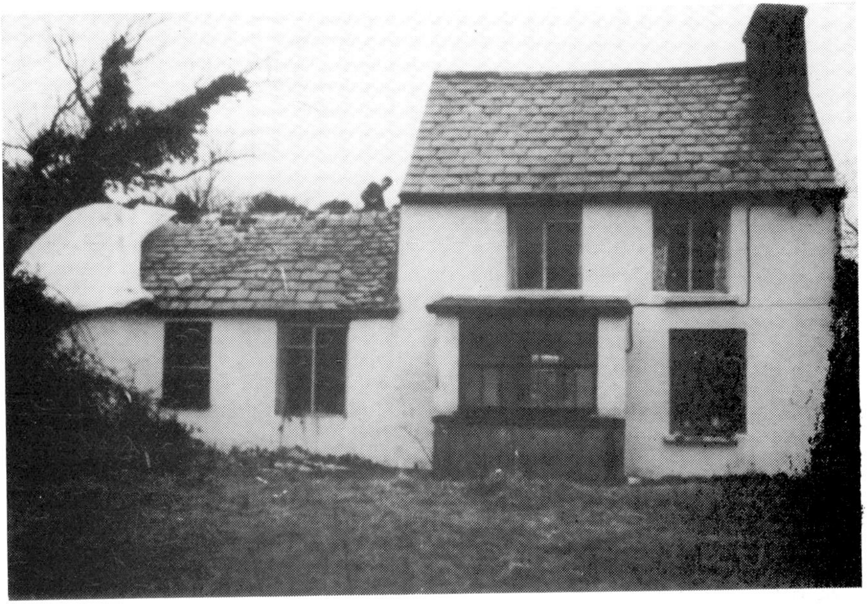

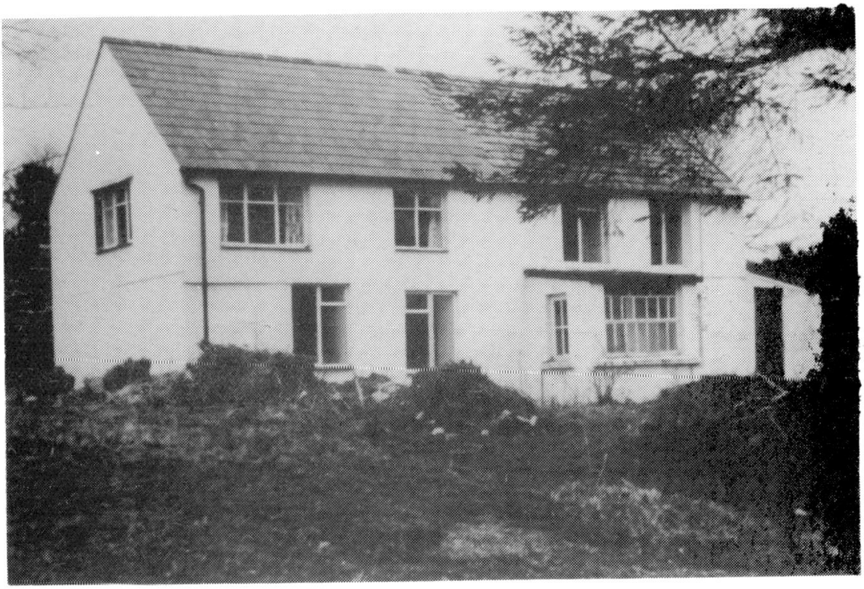

being glad of our custom, they seemed to be punishing us for not having paid them enough. Meal after meal, we were given no choice of dessert — and meal after meal, it was exactly the same: an exceptionally dry and uninspiring slice of Swiss roll. And if we left the Swiss roll, or ate only part of it, the uneaten portion would reappear the next morning for breakfast. Fortunately there was an excellent swimming-pool (even if several of the children did have to be rescued from it); and Malta itself was a delight.

As the children grew older we became more adventurous, holidaying at various times in such places as Altaea, Menorca and Majorca; though we also enjoyed some traditional holidays in England, where we spent a marvellous Easter each year from 1969 to 1972 at the Narracott Hotel at Woolacombe in Devon. There, for around £200 for the whole family, we enjoyed a family room with full board (including afternoon tea for the children), an indoor swimming-pool and a wonderful beach.

Our family caravanning holidays continued, much improved when we traded in our Sprite Major and moved up to the considerable luxury of a six-berth Knowsley. And then in 1977, with the children's ages now ranging from eleven up to sixteen, we realised that it would soon be our last chance for a family holiday which included all six of us, and we organised a major holiday on America's west coast. George Faith of Photoscan, by now a long-standing friend, gave us not only advice but also active help; and soon a 22ft Winnebago motor-home had been reserved for us for a three-week holiday.

After flying to Los Angeles, we stayed briefly with George and his wife Eunice in Laguna, which looked out over the Pacific Ocean to the south of the city; and we made an early morning call on another Photoscan friend, Val Barber, who lived with his wife Dorothy in Anaheim, a prosperous southern suburb. The children were bowled over by the experience of having doughnuts for breakfast and then being able to pick half a sack of grapefruit from a grapefruit tree in the Barbers' garden.

Then we set off in the Winnebago, going north on Highway One. The Winnebago, named after a tribe of American Indians, had facilities far exceeding anything we had ever experienced as European caravanners. It could be linked-up to mains water, electricity and sewage at most of the campsites we visited. It also had comfortable beds and an extremely practical kitchen with an eight cubic foot fridge. As Dorothy was quick to observe, this was larger than the fridge we had at home.

The three weeks went by all too fast. We travelled up north as far as San Francisco, via the wonders of Hearst Castle, the mansion once owned by William Randolph Hearst, on whom Orson Welles modelled his classic Citizen Kane; and Carmel (just south of Monterey) a city which was founded as an art colony and is packed with art galleries and buildings in a wide range of architectural styles. Finally, turning south, we went down to San Diego, on the very edge of Mexico.

Besides these family holidays, Dorothy and I did much travelling alone together. Sometimes this meant us being away from home for a child's birthday; but we have always taken the view that loving one's children very much should not mean that one has to be a martyr to them. Do your duty to your children, and do more than your duty; but remember that you also have a duty to your spouse, with whom you chose to spend your life long before any children came on the scene.

Between 1970 and 1986 we went to no fewer than ten ABTA conferences. These events, and the pre- and post-convention tours which they invariably included, took us to Rotterdam, Cannes, Vienna, Florence, Lisbon, Houston, Phoenix, Los Angeles and Miami, with associated visits to Cyprus and St. Lucia. Once we even went as far as Australia. And a list like this can hardly begin to describe what it was like to be on one of these highly organised visits, on which VIP treatment was taken for granted. Imagine, for example, a banquet given by British Rail on one of their ferries in Rotterdam, a banquet on a scale we had never expected to experience. Imagine being in Cannes, and visiting the Loewes Hotel in Monte Carlo with its fabulous cabaret. Imagine going to the opera and the ballet in Vienna, and sitting down to a banquet for 2,000 people in a Viennese palace.

In 1979 we made the first of our four visits to Canada, where we visited various cousins who gave us a wonderfully warm Canadian welcome all the way across the Continent from Vancouver Island in the west, through Edmonton, Calgary and Winnipeg, to Toronto and Truro in the east.

Another time we took our daughter Janet with us when we visited Sri Lanka — which I still think of as 'Ceylon', as I was taught to do at school. There we visited representations of the Lord Buddha in every conceivable size and situation; and there we also had the disquieting experience of seeing hotels of the most sublime excellence cheek by jowl with the most abject poverty and distress.

We also took Janet with us when we holidayed for a week in Molinella, fourteen miles north-east of Bologna, as the guests of Georgio Lippi. We had met him and his son and daughter as a result of playing host to them when their choir visited Shrewsbury, and Georgio had decided that we in our turn should be royally entertained. His eighty-year-old mother fed us with Italian generosity, and Georgio had us up early every morning to ensure that during our stay we saw not only Molinella, but also numerous other towns and cities, including Bologna, Ravenna (where we saw Pavarotti), and Venice.

Earlier that year, Dorothy and I had travelled to New Orleans where, since he was away, we were able to stay in Glyn Williams's beautiful apartment. We were there for the famous 'Mardi Gras' festival, which was on a scale unlike anything I have encountered anywhere else in the world. The combination of the processions, the displays, the vivid colours and the Jazz playing made it an outstanding experience. It seemed that the whole city was alive with music and goodwill.

That same year, Dorothy used a family bequest to buy a timber chalet for us on the Welsh coast near Aberdovey. We have spent many happy times at 'Curlew', as we call it; though not as many as we had anticipated, because of our travels further afield.

In 1984, for example, we made our first journey to the island of St. Lucia in the Caribbean. I managed to get stung by a jelly-fish, but this did not prevent us from falling in love with the Caribbean. On that first occasion, we made a number of life-long friends. These included Dave and Heather Niles, whom we visited soon afterwards at their home in Guernsey; and later the same year we had the perfect excuse for returning to the Caribbean for a second visit: our friend Jack Jameson, who had just lost his lovely wife Vera, urgently needed companions for a holiday. So we accompanied him to Discovery Bay in Barbados. Since then we have made at least four further visits to Barbados, and we hope to go there many more times before we die.

Indeed our first cruise started from Barbados. A week on the *Ocean Islander* was quite enough to infect us with the cruising bug, and since then we have also gone cruising on the *Cunard Countess*, the *Crown Dynasty* and the *Sea Ward*. By this means we have travelled to St Martin, Grenada, St. Thomas, Antigua, Puerto Rica and St. Kitts in the Caribbean; and we spent another week on the *Ocean Islander* in the eastern Mediterranean, starting from Venice, calling in at the mediaeval walled city of Dubrovnik, and sailing on through the Corinth Canal and across the Aegean Sea and the Sea of Marmara all the way to Istanbul. The following year we cruised the western Mediterranean in the QE2, a voyage which began with a memorable crossing of the Bay of Biscay in a Force Eight gale.

Cruising is certainly hard to beat. There is usually excellent food and plenty of it. There are many interesting people, and plenty of time to talk to them. And almost every day one arrives in some new and interesting place, having brought one's travelling hotel along, so that there is no need for constant packing and unpacking: the bane of any touring holiday on dry land.

We have had numerous other holidays, but I will only mention one more: a sentimental journey made just two years ago to celebrate Dorothy's 60th birthday. We went back to Southern Ireland where we had been on honeymoon so many years before; and we also found the time to visit the grave of our old friend and business partner Jim Manson.

CHAPTER THIRTEEN

As our interests in the management and development of property continued to grow, so did the size of our building division.

Some of our projects were small but very satisfying. For example, we purchased Jane's Place in Coton Hill for £275 freehold, as the result of an advertisement in the local press. After renovating it with the aid of grants from the local Council we enjoyed a reasonable rental income for a number of years before selling it for £14,750. Again, we purchased 66 Ellesmere Road, tidied up the house and then sold it, excluding the adjoining land, for only a little more than we had paid for it. But a few years later we sold that adjoining land as a building plot and so made a handsome profit. We also purchased St. Nicholas's Church for only £18,000, fully intending to turn it into an hotel. Another still larger project came on stream instead; but we still did very well, selling St. Nicholas's for 2½ times what we had paid for it.

Our sale of the Crewe Hotel site had left us with substantial funds in hand, so we acquired the historic 73 Wyle Cop, a timber-framed Grade 1 listed building which required complete renovation. Plans were drawn up by my brilliant young architectural adviser Alan Snell. Curiously enough, he and his wife Jan had rented one of our flats on their return from South Africa, but it had been several years before I realised his value and drew him into the business, setting up a small drawing office for him, and making him our Building Development Manager.

73 Wyle Cop provided work for our building division for eighteen months; and it also turned out to be a much more interesting project than we had thought. The point was that as we began taking it apart, we discovered that it was a much older and more interesting building than anyone had supposed: indeed, it was an elegant early fifteenth-century merchants' house of sophisticated timber frame construction. In order to preserve and display that timber frame, Alan had to go back to the drawing-board and start again.

We had received substantial grants towards the restoration and I am proud to say that when the work was completed according to Alan's new specifications we also won a number of prestigious awards. The end product was three shops and three flats, all of which rapidly found tenants. The flats we retained for many years before selling them leasehold. The three shops and the freehold of the property we have to this day.

Another project which was good for us, though it did not have such a happy ending, concerned a Chapel together with a little house that we purchased in Beacalls Lane. Initially I had thought of the Chapel as a handy warehouse property close to the town centre; but on running a tape-measure across it, I realised that there was enough room for two squash courts and all the necessary facilities. We carried out a very economical conversion, and (thanks to a little publicity) by the time we opened our new squash club we had an almost complete membership.

The club was operated by membership cards and by coin-in-the-slot systems which controlled both the lights and the booking arrangements. This meant that it could be left almost permanently unmanned, with staff visiting just once a day to collect the money and clean the premises.

'Before' and 'After' photos of 73 Wyle Cop

However we had no member of staff who wanted to occupy the little house that went alongside the club; and we did not want to create a tenancy which we might have difficulty in terminating. So we decided to sell the entire property freehold, with the squash club as a going concern. We therefore placed small classified advertisements in *The Daily Express* and *The Daily Telegraph*. These brought us approximately forty replies and we decided to sell to the first person who agreed our price. When that person dropped out, only ten days before we were due to go abroad on holiday, we contacted the next people on the list and explained the situation. If they still wanted to buy the property, they would have to exchange contracts within seven days, and the only way to do that would be to get the two lots of solicitors together. This was agreed, and the sale went through smoothly.

However, as soon as they had completed the purchase, they applied for a licence to sell alcohol on the premises. Clearly this involved employing a full-time member of staff for whom, in the quiet periods, the presence of alcohol must have been a severe temptation. At any rate the new arrangements were not a success, and after a while the club closed down. Since then it has passed through several hands, and at the time of writing it is once again empty and for sale.

A more unusual and most demanding project was the Howard Street Warehouse, a handsome Georgian canal warehouse and butter-market which had been allowed to deteriorate to a point at which its owners, British Rail, wanted to demolish it to make room for a car park. However the Shrewsbury Civic Society fought successfully at a public inquiry to save it from demolition, and we then bought it for a comparatively small sum.

The Howard Street Warehouse, now the Buttermarket

There was clearly a great future for the Howard Street Warehouse, and in the early stages of the work we made good use of the new Job Creation scheme to recruit fifteen boys (unskilled and often illiterate) who worked enthusiastically under the inspirational leadership of Wally Jones. Our intention had been to put in management and run the centre ourselves; but as that moment drew closer and closer I could see that it would be very demanding and, having had one nervous breakdown, I did not wish to risk another by over-reaching myself.

It was at this critical juncture that Kerry Wycherley turned up on my doorstep and virtually begged me to sell. He had developed a night-club in Wrexham and thought that he now had the experience to produce something outstanding in the Howard Street premises. He was clearly the right man for the job. I sold out to him very gladly and at a good profit; and in due course he produced a night-club, known as the Buttermarket, which is a credit to him and has been a great success in the town.

It was a relief to be able to concentrate upon my most ambitious project to date. But perhaps I should start at the beginning.

In 1978, the Area Hospital Authority had completed a grand new hospital on the outskirts of Shrewsbury and had moved out of the Royal Salop Infirmary. The RSI, as it is usually known, was then boarded up and left rather like the hulk of a huge liner which had sailed down river and become stranded. The Hospital Authority was obliged to offer it to all the various government offices, but it was in a run-down condition and no-one wanted to have anything to do with it.

Eventually in May 1979 it was offered for public sale by informal tender. By this time Dorothy and I had decided that we were going to take life more quietly and were not going to take on any more large projects. However we couldn't resist making what we regarded as a very modest offer for the whole complex, which included not only the RSI building but the adjoining Nurses' Home.

By August, when we had left for a visit to Canada, we had still had no decision. We therefore arranged for a telegram to be sent as soon as the answer was known. The telegram duly arrived, and it was worded as arranged: "The baby has arrived". This meant that our purchase price had been agreed. We immediately set the wheels in motion for the purchase of the property and for obtaining the necessary planning consents.

The work in this connection would have been too much for our one-man drawing-office to contemplate; but this problem was solved by Alan Snell going into partnership with Andrew Arrol, the Shrewsbury and Atcham Borough Council (SABC) Conservation Officer. As soon as we had possession of the property they set up their office in the premises of the RSI. However gaining possession of the property took far longer than expected.

In November 1979 we were able to put in a planning application to convert the RSI into 30 flats on the upper floors, in a development to be known as *The Court* Flats; with sixteen shops on the ground floor and twelve workshop-shops on the level below. The SABC gave its consent in February 1980; but at that stage we still had no signed contract with the vendors, and for many months we faced a serious risk of being gazumped by some other property developer.

The problem was that the site had been put together over some 150 years. It consisted of no fewer than eleven original hereditaments. Each of them had been vested in the

Area Health Authority, but a number of the deeds had been lost. Eventually the difficulty was resolved by persuading a number of elderly gentlemen to come out of retirement to sign depositions to the effect that the Health Authority had been in unquestioned ownership and occupation.

Finally at the end of March 1980 we were able to exchange contracts and complete our purchase; and work began the very next day.

In the interim the building had been a magnet for thieves and vandals; and I had begun touring the site, especially at weekends, armed only with my camera and a telephoto lens. I never had to take a picture: it was enough to point the camera at intruders for them to disappear as if by magic.

In February I had also spent one of the coldest days of my life, mainly in the dark, making a detailed inspection of the boarded-up building from top to bottom. Apart from being cold it was very sinister. I went through every corner of the RSI, from the south wing where the ghost of a grey lady was said to have served tea to patients, to the operating theatres which had been vacated once the last operations had been completed.

A good deal of equipment had been left behind, some of which we were able to sell to veterinary practices. In fact one of the first things we did after completing the purchase was to hold a sale of redundant equipment. This unexpectedly yielded a substantial sum, including as it did the complete lead lining of the whole of the X-ray department, a good deal of kitchen equipment and a number of portable buildings which had been erected on the periphery of the site.

Having started at the relatively salubrious top of the building, we worked down to the lower levels where we were entirely dependent upon torchlight. On the lowest level of all we came to the kitchen where the revolting stench in that enclosed space was almost more than we could bear. No-one had made a thorough clearance of perishable foods when the kitchen was abandoned, let alone given it a proper cleaning; and after so many months the smell of decay was indescribably awful. At this level of the building we were also faced with the presence of large quantities of asbestos. To deal with this we would have to train men, kit them out with special equipment and comply with a complicated set of regulations regarding disposal.

Knowing that I would need to devote most of my time to this new project, I engaged Gordon Menhinick to manage our other activities, especially the industrial estates. I then engaged John Hingley, a building surveyor, to help me at the RSI. In practice John Hingley did not stay with me for long, so that the work at the RSI was shared between Gordon and myself. Fortunately this led to a very happy bond between us. We were united for some eight years as employer and employee, for longer than that as landlord and tenant, and for still longer as personal friends.

Gordon had an office on the premises and his presence, combined with that of the architects, helped make it possible for us to make substantial savings by re-using materials from parts of the property which were demolished. This included steelwork from the boiler houses, which was re-fabricated to provide the main structure for the central roof section.

There was a good deal of demolition to be done, as we were determined to remove everything that had been added to the building since 1910: including the pipe-work that the NHS had festooned over the front of the building, and the sluice block and extra floor they had tacked on at the back which had completely ruined the building's architectural balance.

As for restoration: the plan was to complete the new roof and the installation of whatever mains services were needed, and then to create the new flats from the top floor working down, with priority to be given to a show flat. This scheme was a success and we rapidly agreed the sale of a number of flats from the plans alone.

Suddenly there was a good deal of interest in our conservation work, and I was very touched by an article in *Building* magazine headed 'Saviour of Shrewsbury' in which it was said that I had 'done more than any other single person to save attractive old buildings in Shrewsbury'.

Indeed, everything seemed to be going extremely well when to our horror we discovered dry rot in some units immediately beneath flats which were nearing completion. This was a very nasty blow. Dry rot in a building is like cancer in a human being, and completely eradicating it involved us in a huge amount of extra work and expenditure before we were able to recoup some of our costs from the completed flats. The situation was made still more serious by the fact that the bank borrowing rate shot up to 18% and stayed there for some considerable time. One of the early flat purchasers even had to be accommodated for several weeks at our expense in a local hotel because we were unable to give her possession of her flat on the due date.

The strain became so intense that in 1981 I suffered a second nervous breakdown, and had to have an extensive period off work.

CHAPTER FOURTEEN

Troubles often seem to come together; and it was while I was still recuperating that the North Shropshire District Council finally decided to deal with my lack of planning consents for the Rosehill Estate by serving enforcement orders.

Fortunately Gordon Menhinick and Dorothy between them managed to hold the fort, and in due course some good came out of it. So often apparent disasters turn out to be for the best. Because once I was back in harness again, I was able to pin down the NSDC on what they would like us to do in return for having the enforcement orders withdrawn. I then arranged for the necessary work. It was extremely expensive, but in due course we were granted full planning consent on a progressive basis for the whole estate. The problem of fifteen-year renewals was removed, the long-term future of the estate was assured, and of course its value rose considerably.

The extent to which attitudes have changed over the last thirty years is quite instructive. We began by being treated virtually as public enemies, providing facilities for businesses in whom the authorities had little or no interest. Now we are positively encouraged, receiving grants for providing small factories and workshops in which entrepreneurs can create jobs in the rural areas in which we operate. Curiously enough, our original brochure used the slogan: 'Come to the Country, where Small Firms Grow'.

In my absence, Gordon and Dorothy had also maintained the momentum of the work at the old RSI. At its peak there were fifty people employed on this project including specialist stonemason contractors and stone cleaners. The decline in the property market resulted in the last flat not being sold until 1983, by which time our work was well advanced on what was to be called the Parade Shopping Centre on the lowest two floors.

Although certain areas had to be judiciously screened from view, the whole project was formally opened on 13 June 1983 by the Duke of Gloucester; and before long all twenty-five of the new shops were occupied. Some were outstandingly successful, moving from smaller to larger premises either within the Parade or elsewhere in Shrewsbury. Inevitably, others fell by the wayside, and of course retirement has resulted in some changes of ownership; but I am glad to say that the majority of the original businesses which were there on the opening day are still there today.

However it hasn't all been plain sailing; and we had one major conflict with the Local Authority, who served an enforcement notice in an effort to prevent us from using the space in front of the building for car-parking. They wanted us to turn it instead into a recreation area complete with seats and flower-beds. We pulled out all the stops to fight this change, believing that it would be the kiss of death for The Parade. A petition was organised and we pointed out in very plain language that this area had been used for car parking virtually since cars had been invented. Fortunately we were successful. The car park is now one of the most appreciated amenities in the centre of Shrewsbury, besides providing four people with happy part-time employment and creating substantial revenue.

In order to guarantee the good maintenance of the old RSI, we established a separate company, two of whose directors are nominated by the leaseholders of the Court Flats. There have been so many case histories of landlords being unwilling to fulfil their responsibilities that leaseholders are often naturally sceptical about arrangements of this sort. However I believe that the majority of our leaseholders recognise that we have managed to keep maintenance charges relatively low, while keeping the standards so high that there is a sustained demand for any flats which come up for sale. This is of course very much in the leaseholders' own interests.

As a company, we made only very modest profits out of the Court flats; but we created the Parade Shopping Centre at an economical cost, and we still had in hand the neighbouring Nurses' Home, together with some surplus land. However we were rather at a loss about how to proceed, because we had no real wish to invest any greater proportion of our limited funds in this area of the town. We did incur modest costs in examining various possibilities such as a multi-storey car park and a major retail development, but none of them came to fruition, chiefly because there was a noticeable down-turn in the world of commercial building.

For several years we simply had to bide our time; and then within a few months of each other *McCarthy and Stone* and *Anglia Homes*, two leaders in the field of retirement homes, both expressed an interest in the site, which their local representatives appeared to regard as an outstanding opportunity. We were on tenter-hooks when one of the two dropped out. We were told by the other that although it would take a few months to obtain the approval of the board, this would only be a formality.

In the meantime a local developer who had a number of successful projects to his

The restored frontage

credit became aware of the site and set his heart on it. When we told him the price he said that he was prepared to match it; but we told him in good faith that although a contract had not yet been exchanged, we were substantially committed to another buyer.

At that moment the board of the national company vetoed the project, so we were almost back to square one. However, knowing of the competition for the site had made the local man keen; and before long he had signed a contract with us, the purchase had been completed, and we had our money.

Although strictly speaking what happened next to the Nurses' Home is not part of my autobiography, I must tell you the twist in this particular tale. Dramatic changes in the property market affected some of the buyer's other projects, with the result that his bankers withdrew their support. His company was forced into liquidation, his personal guarantees were called in, and the result was that the bank became the owners of the property. After sustained marketing over an extended period they eventually had no option but to accept less than a third of the price for which we had sold it. Then before the sale was completed, there was a serious fire at the Nurses' Home. The intending purchasers could reasonably have expected to benefit from the subsequent insurance claim, but at the last minute there was a competitive bid from someone who was willing to take the property subject to fire damage. This meant that if they wanted the property they had no option but to complete on similar terms, which they did. This part of the story at least has a happy ending, for Shropshire Homes Ltd. have done a superb restoration, creating twenty-seven apartments which have turned an eyesore into an outstanding property.

of the old RSI

Incidentally, I have mentioned my occasional difficulties with Local Authorities, but I have always recognised their importance; and although in my early fifties I was still a very unpolitical person, I started to feel some guilt about how little I had contributed in that sphere. Then in March 1982 came the famous moment when the 'Gang of Four' (Roy Jenkins, David Owen, William Rodgers and Shirley Williams) broke away from the Labour Party to form the Social Democratic Party (SDP). They seemed to be just what I was looking for: a group of people who supported sensible middle-of-the-road policies, and I gave them my enthusiastic support.

This led to my standing as an SDP candidate in local elections both for the Shrewsbury and Atcham Borough Council, and for the Uffington Parish Council. Failing to get elected was not a severe disappointment, though several years later I was very disillusioned by the break in the alliance between David Owen of the SDP and David Steel of the Liberal Party, and my political aspirations went back to square one.

As for my unsuccessful election campaign: my principal recollection is of my attempt to canvass a blue-rinse lady. She opened her door to me, but cut short my opening remarks with the words: "Young man, I have voted Conservative all my life, and I always will!" Politically there was clearly no point in pursuing the argument; but I couldn't help feeling just a little pleased at being called a 'young man' at the age of 52!

CHAPTER FIFTEEN

By 1987, we were ready for a new project; and when (as a result of a nationwide over-capacity in the brewing industry) the Ditherington Maltings was put up for sale, I thought it fitted the bill ideally.

The point was that the Maltings was a Grade 1 listed building, with 120,000 square feet of buildings on $3^1/_8$ acres of land. Not only would it make an excellent business park, but it was in an ideal location, only a mile from our head office, and half-a-mile from the town centre, the Postal sorting office and the Railway Station. By chance it also adjoined a property we already owned on the main Shrewsbury to Whitchurch road.

It would also fit extremely well into our property portfolio. By this time we already had substantial investments in rented retail and industrial property; but we didn't want to do any more retail development because with a number of large new developments in the pipeline we could see that Shrewsbury was in danger of having too many shops for the available business. We were also reluctant to increase our investment in rented residential property because of the increase in management costs. So a new business park would be the ideal way forward, especially when we could see a potential annual rental income in excess of £600,000.

So we tendered for the property, and when our tender as accepted we completed the purchase and instructed architects. Personally I felt over the moon. Not only was the Maltings an outstanding property for which substantial grants were available, but also the project would take some three years to complete; and at the age of 59, and with Philip and Jonathan both established in the firm, I was happy for it to be my swan-song.

Very soon I had nine tenants lined up to take possession as soon as the restoration was complete. This was extremely encouraging, as I had always found that it was the first few tenants for any new scheme who were the difficult ones to find, as in effect they were taking a risk on our ability to deliver. Fortunately the successful completion of the old RSI project had considerably enhanced our reputation.

However there was one factor which I had not taken into account. The local Director of Planning had decided to take early retirement, and was about to be replaced by a new broom.

Now we had deliberately split our plans into three phases, not only because that was the way in which we had constructed our schedule of work, but also because if any part of the plans should be considered unacceptable by the planners, that part could be resubmitted without prejudicing the whole scheme. However, at the only meeting I ever had with him, the new Director of Planning decided that he would only accept a comprehensive application to include all the proposed activities on the entire site. In doing so he crossed swords with his own officers, and utterly dismayed our architects. The result was that the meeting broke up without any progress having been made.

Eventually we would get planning consent for everything for which we had asked in the first place; but it would take us four years. By that time we had lost all nine of our original prospective tenants, the market had changed beyond all recognition, I was four years older and looking retirement firmly in the face and we had personal and company problems which had not existed four years previously.

One of these problems was that the Inland Revenue had chosen us as the target of a tax inquiry; and the rules of such an inquiry are heavily loaded against the victim. For a start, we had to pay the cost of our accountants producing detailed information going back over seven years to satisfy the Inland Revenue's inquiries, and that alone came to £60,000. Next, the inquiry was a blight on our business over a period of eighteen months. Finally, we were asked to pay some £350,000 in additional tax and penalties which they considered themselves very generous in allowing us to pay in three instalments.

There was another serious problem connected with tax. Since my days with Jim Manson as a garage proprietor we had been quite rightly treated as a trading company. This meant that on my death or retirement, my investment in the company would be subject to business relief at 50%. However over the years our activities had progressively changed, and most of our dealings were now in investment property. We argued that we were not an ordinary property investment company of the type which simply lets properties to tenants on long full-repairing leases. We not only created our properties, but also continued to be directly involved in their management and maintenance. However, this argument was to no avail. We were told that we would be treated as an investment company, and so could not qualify for business tax relief. We were also told that to qualify for such relief at least 50% of our income must come from a trading activity. So, with our Maltings project on hold, I channelled my efforts into finding a solution to this problem.

It happened that two miles out of town a company with foreign backing had begun restoring and extending an existing property to create a 60-room nursing home. They had spent over £900,000 on it, but we were able to buy it from them for just over £500,000, and were quite prepared to spend a further £800,000 completing the project. Our intention was to put proper management in place, making use of our building expertise both to complete and to maintain the property. Nor had I overlooked the fact that our daughter Janet would almost certainly have all the necessary qualifications to be a part of this new business in due course.

Our building division did many months of work on the nursing home and I felt that we were really making excellent progress. However, even as the work was being done, the market in nursing and residential care was rapidly changing. In particular the regulations were getting stricter, which made both the capital and the running costs much higher. Also, most of the potential patients were paid for by local authorities, who were prepared to pay less and less for them. The result was that very high levels of occupancy were necessary to reach break-even; and a large number of under-capitalised small nursing homes of fewer than twenty rooms were being forced into liquidation, with their assets fetching very little on the open market.

I still took the view that our project was large enough to be economically viable; but our accountants were certain that the risks were too great, and I felt that I had no option but to abort the project.

We put the property on the market and within a month we had an offer of £750,000. I now wish that we had accepted. In practice we continued to own the property for several years, with all the costs which that involved; and only now do we anticipate its sale for an amount which is substantially less than the offer which we turned down.

CHAPTER SIXTEEN

I recently heard an outstanding sportsman declare that he learned less from his victories than from his defeats. His message was that a winner never knows whether he could still do better, and by how much; while a loser who knows that he has done all he can, has a very clear idea by how much he must improve to equal or exceed the winner. It's certainly no good giving up when things go wrong. You will remember that Jim and I suffered a severe setback after the price of new cars was cut back in 1959, and lost some £20,000 before the market righted itself. However this was what had spurred us on to diversify, and what had therefore led to the creation both of Q-Hire and of the highly successful Stonemanson.

We had our share of failures, including the lorry firm founded to work on the Treweryn Dam, and Shilphone Agricultural Ltd, each of which lost us around £2,000 at 1960s prices. Fortunately the only other company we had to put into receivership was Coral Pools Ltd. Once again there was a personal loss of some £2,000; but we were able to pay our creditors 12s/6d in the pound, and (as I mentioned) my management of the company gave me the confidence to build our own swimming-pool. Originally intended as a facility for the children, it still provides our home with an outstanding amenity, and I am sure that my regular early-morning swim has been a major factor in maintaining my own good health.

In any case, nothing ventured nothing gained; and each of these unsuccessful projects initially appeared to be just as promising as others which succeeded. I sometimes think that even those companies which failed might have been made to succeed had they been our sole activity and engaged all our attention. But the hard fact of life is that one cannot do everything oneself, and the biggest factor in commercial success is to master the most important and difficult art of delegation.

One must also remember that sometimes one has to pay to learn. For example, becoming Young Engineer of Great Britain in partnership with young Legge was an undoubted feather in John's cap. Legge's father Mr. Ingram Legge clearly believed that the equipment which our sons had developed as a school project had commercial potential, and I was keen to support John in a field in which I felt he had special abilities. So we and the Legges put up enough money to gain substantial backing for the project from 3I, a public company which invests in small firms. However, as I mentioned in an earlier chapter, Ingram Legge, in an extended bout of administrative activity, had very soon absorbed all the new company's resources, some £90,000. We had been persuaded to guarantee half a bank loan to extend the abortive activity. The net result was that I personally lost a grand total of £12,000 an expensive lesson.

Tax savings have been another bait used to part us from our money. Fortunately most of the schemes in which I have invested have been very worthwhile. However, there have been exceptions. For example, I was once persuaded to invest heavily in a housing Business Expansion Scheme (BES) sponsored by Allied Dunbar. We were told by their financial consultants that there were so many advantages that it was virtually impossible for us to lose. Not only would we get an immediate credit against tax of 40% of our investment, but that investment was guaranteed against any capital loss beyond a nominal 5%.

Allied Dunbar had also produced an impressive brochure showing expected annual profits of 45%. So even if we discounted their figures by 50%, we would still end up with a net profit of 22.5% per annum. To make matters worse, we were encouraged to borrow a substantial part of the investment through a financial scheme also set up by Allied Dunbar, whose advantage was that the interest charged was tax-deductible.

During the five-year period of the BES scheme, the property market went down substantially. The insurance on our capital investment in the property was still 100% all right; but unfortunately what we didn't realise was that so many people were taking their cut out of both the rental earnings and the capital assets that when one combined those costs with the interest on our loan, that unhappy episode cost us (depending on how the figures are interpreted) somewhere between £25,000 and £35,000: another expensive lesson.

There is another BES marketing scheme on which I am still reserving judgment. I invested £20,000 less an immediate tax credit of 40%, making a net investment of £12,000. My reasons for investing were solidly based, as I thought, on my belief in a man with an outstanding marketing talent in the sphere of leisure and sporting activities, a sphere which I believed had substantial growth potential. In practice he has been subject to one crisis after another, but he has survived in spite of everything, so I still hope that I will get my investment back and may even make a substantial profit. However as I write these words my investment is certainly not realisable, so I feel that I should include this story in my chapter of unpleasant lessons.

Another expensive mistake was made when we installed a goods lift from the service entrance to the main upper floor of the *Parade Shopping Centre*. We realised that we had failed to research the matter adequately, because the 50% of the shops on the lower level never needed to use it, while the 50% on the upper level found it just as easy to bring goods in by one of the other three entrances. The net cost to us was £5,000 for the lift, together with the costs first of installing it and then, when it was found to be redundant, of removing it again.

Stocks and shares are still more of a gamble. We once invested £2,000 in the shares of a firm called Kelt Energy. Our decision was based on a tip (probably fourth or fifth-hand) that all sorts of wonderful things were going to happen to its shares, then priced at a very modest fifty pence per share. The shares then went up a little before going down a lot. Oil wells either failed to produce any oil at all, or did so in quantities too small to recover the costs of drilling. Eventually the company was subject to what was politely called a 'reconstruction', under whose terms we would receive one large 'new' share for every fifty of our small 'old' ones. We hoped that 'reconstruction' implied rebuilding and coming good. However, after a further long wait, our 'new' shares turned out to be worth only seven pence each. Our £2,000 investment had therefore been 'reconstructed' into £5-60.

I will mention just two more ventures, one of which failed rapidly, the other of which had been a great success for many years but succumbed to changing market conditions.

The one which failed rapidly was 'Seeds of Friendship'. I have always been interested in direct mail, and I had tested the water in a modest way with Western Picture Library back in the 1970s. The idea behind 'Seeds of Friendship' was that seeds could be posted economically to anywhere in the world, and would make ideal presents to mark almost any occasion, from a cheerful event like a birthday, a christening or a promotion, to a more sombre occasion like a bereavement or a divorce. I hoped that it would give me a part-time interest during my retirement; and I also thought that it was a unique concept which had the commercial potential for world-wide direct mailing.

In due course I went into partnership with the Bickertons, a husband and wife team who seemed enthusiastic, had a great deal of marketing experience and did a good job in producing a most attractive product. We opened a small office which I was quite confident would have to be very quickly extended, and started placing advertisements in national newspapers and magazines.

The success or failure of 'Seeds of Friendship' depended entirely upon getting enough response from the advertisements to justify their cost. I remain confident that if only we could have passed break-even, we could have developed into a major market force. Unfortunately, although those who used our service wrote of it with great enthusiasm, the moment came when I could not risk pouring more money into sustaining the advertising. 'Seeds of Friendship' was therefore one of my more substantial disappointments; and although I was able to set my losses against taxed income, it cost me a hurtful £12,000.

The company which had done well but which eventually failed was Travelon. Our profit margins were eroded by price-cutting competition from retail travel agencies owned by the tour operators; and eventually, after three years of losses, we sold out for a tenth of what we could have obtained only five years previously.

Over the years we have inevitably had our fair share of bad debts and staff fraud; and I should finally mention that I minimised our bad debts by acting as our own credit controller for most of the time that I ran the company. My object was always to help my customers to avoid getting too deeply into my debt. If they couldn't pay everything, I would try to persuade them to pay half. If even that was impossible, I tried to get them to agree to a series of payments phased over several months. The point was that if someone got too deeply into my debt, he was likely to go to another supplier. That meant that I would lose the customer as well as risking the loss of the whole sum owed to me.

All in all, these errors and unhappy episodes must have cost us well over one million pounds in hard cash, not to mention the vast amount of unrewarded work which went into trying to contain the losses. One has to pay for one's learning, and of course I had chosen to terminate my formal education somewhat prematurely at only thirteen years of age.

Sometimes I wonder whether I would have been more or less successful had I completed my schooling and possibly gone on to higher education. But then I would probably have been expected to join some established institution. I suppose that, having made my own choice to leave school, I always felt the need to prove that I had done the right thing; and to some extent I have always expected to have to learn the hard way. Looking back, however, I can honestly say that in spite of all the difficulties I have no regrets.

CHAPTER SEVENTEEN

Almost as soon as I had written the last words of Chapter Sixteen, I realised that I must qualify those 'no regrets'. Higher education would have made me more confident in the use of my own language, and more able to appreciate my literary heritage. I should also have liked to be more confident in a few foreign languages. Last but not least, I should have liked to receive a better musical education. It is language and music which, more than anything else, enable us both to communicate with others and to enhance our understanding of the world around us.

It strikes me as curious that most ancient civilisations were based upon slavery; and in today's world, although we certainly don't believe in slavery any more, we are the ones in danger of becoming slaves to our own machines. As in many other spheres, the middle road is probably the right road; and I have no doubt that meaningful work is vital for any man or woman who wishes to be completely fulfilled.

Indeed I am convinced that unless one happens to be very ill or very old it is positively damaging to be paid for doing nothing. We are to a large extent what we do; and if we do nothing we tend to become a nobody. If this is allowed to happen for any sustained length of time, our self-esteem is damaged. Bad habits are easily formed; and it takes a person of quite outstanding character to want to start regular work after an extended period of doing nothing.

However we have allowed our society to develop in such a way that we have millions of unemployed. To me, this represents a major failing on our part. My point is that there are numerous ways of improving our environment and the way in which we live, which are commercially uneconomical. So if someone is unemployed because there is no full-time job available in his or her specialised field, I believe it would be better for that person to be asked to do some socially or environmentally useful task than to be paid for doing nothing.

However high someone's previous level of attainment, he or she will find satisfaction and even increased self-knowledge in functioning at some lower level for a period. There is no reason why doing some comparatively mundane task should prejudice anyone's gaining employment in his or her own line when it comes along. In fact most people in their younger days have had some experience of the lower levels of semi-skilled or even unskilled employment, often in hotels or fast-food establishments. Practical experience in the best teacher, and the wider that experience the better.

I can also see that very soon the time will come when it is thought desirable for retired people to contribute some activity for the good of the community. It already stands out a mile that, in retirement, the happy people are the busy people.

I would apply this principle even to those who have reached extreme old age and must of necessity spend their declining years in rest-homes or nursing-homes. There is nothing more depressing than going into a nursing-home and seeing all the residents sitting round in their chairs saying nothing and doing nothing, except perhaps waiting for the next meal or the next bowel movement. For some this may be an inevitable part of old age; but it is also true that an unused muscle or nerve or brain rapidly becomes unusable. In our extreme old age we should be allowed and encouraged to continue to take part. Whether it is a matter of tending a patch of garden, sweeping a path, arranging flowers, dusting mantel-pieces, winding clocks, sewing on buttons, drawing, painting, or making things for our children and grand-children, there are one-thousand-and-one things for us to do. Even if we get in the way of the staff, please allow us to keep doing something, so that more of us are able to keep our faculties to our dying day.

CHAPTER EIGHTEEN

Religion has been on our minds since before we blundered out of obscurity and aspired to a modicum of civilisation. Born and brought up to be a conventional Church of England Christian, I rapidly found it difficult to believe much of what I was taught during the C of E's endlessly repetitious church services. I agreed that there must be a power vastly greater than ourselves. But I also came to the conclusion that this power, this creator, this God, must be the same not only for Catholics and Protestants, but also for Muslims, Hindus and Buddhists. Our particular teacher and prophet, Jesus Christ, was sufficiently ahead of His time to recognise that there was need of a philosophy based on something more than greed, conquest and the survival of the fittest. I don't doubt that from earliest times there have been excellent mothers and fathers; but it was a revolution for someone to teach things like: 'Suffer the little children to come unto me', and 'Blessed are the meek, for they shall inherit the earth'.

My very practical mind finds it most difficult to accept the traditional idea of miracles. However it is an undoubted miracle that, despite all the sins and deviations of our churches and their ministers over the past 2,000 years, Christianity has survived and spread around the world. I therefore gladly respect and venerate Jesus Christ.

For most of those 2,000 years, Christian preachers have given us the two options of Heaven or Hell; but more recently Hell appears to have been quietly phased out. This leaves us with the tricky problem of our bodies ascending into Heaven, there to join Jesus and the heavenly host and our nearest and dearest. Having given a lot of thought to this, I am confident that when my heart stops pumping, my body will become redundant and, having been cremated or buried or both, is no longer of any significance. It is certainly agreeable to think that people may remember us, and we hope that they will remember us kindly, and that they may even benefit from that remembrance. But I believe firmly in immortality, and therefore I consider that it is very important for us to lead the best lives we can. Because the most important part of us is our brain.

During life, it is our brain which makes our body do everything from looking after us and our family, to constructing a building or writing a sonnet; and our brain is also what makes us uniquely ourselves. But in addition to this (and quite apart from the genetic seed with which most of us try to reproduce ourselves physically) the brain produces the spiritual and intellectual seed which we try to plant in others. Much of this seed falls by the wayside, as in the Parable of the Sower; but there is always some which takes root.

The major recipients of this intellectual seed are of course our children and our children's children in their formative years; and there are individuals such as teachers who have particularly outstanding opportunities for passing on their intellectual seed, even if some of them fail to take full advantage of their opportunity. This is one of the ways in which we are all part of the evolution of our unique species. For in my view we are more than brothers and sisters: we are all part of each other. And how fortunate we are to be part of the great miracle of life itself, life which includes not only the birds, the fishes and the animals but Homo Sapiens, with a great collective brain capable of achieving almost anything.

CHAPTER NINETEEN

My hope is that I have quite a lot more life to come, although I know that throughout most of recorded history I would have been very lucky to have lived as long as I have lived already. What have I achieved in this life? I have played a major part in creating a number of businesses which in their turn have built places in which hundreds of people have lived and worked. In so doing, I have helped to restore and preserve many significant buildings; and during the 50 years of my active working life I have helped to create satisfying work for hundreds of people.

I still have aspirations, and my mind remains active. Indeed, although I get real satisfaction from the small charity I have created, I suffer some frustration from the fact that my mind continues to produce schemes which I am certain are viable and worthwhile projects, though I am aware that at my age I can no longer become involved in the nuts and bolts of building new businesses. It would be wonderful to find an organisation prepared to benefit from my ideas and experience.

Last and most important of all I have my family. Family life is something of which I have vast experience and about which I have strong feelings. Marriage between a compatible man and woman is more than just a union, and can be the most rewarding partnership in the world. Speaking from personal experience, I can state that every aspect of that partnership can improve and mature with age. In that process, with good fortune, it can produce a family headed by two different but complementary people. Not only is this worthwhile in itself, but it is the most efficient unit ever invented for the housing, feeding, guiding, training, comforting and sustaining of a group of people.

Throughout history, premature death frequently created widowers, widows and orphans, to whose aid the larger family could rally. Now there are individuals who lightly enter into single parenthood, sometimes to satisfy a maternal instinct, sometimes for selfish reasons, and frequently as a result of financial pressures.

Yet I believe that the average child needs and deserves the care and interest of a pair of parents to aid its balanced introduction to the great wide world. The drift away from the family is therefore inflicting terrible damage upon our society.

I do not base these views primarily upon Christian values, but there is no doubt that something lightly entered into tends to be more lightly set asunder when it suits us; and it is very much to our advantage if we follow the examples and precedents which have been established for us. A church ceremony with all the trimmings is a wonderful way of formalising the most important contract in two people's lives.

Sadly, changing attitudes towards the significance of the family have become the biggest single factor in the failure of children to clear their first educational hurdles, and in their becoming progressively more and more difficult to teach. This in turns leads to many teachers becoming disillusioned.

At the end of school-days or higher education, the young person damaged by the break-up of the family unit is often unable or unwilling to accept employment at the bottom of the ladder. As a result many of them fail to discover the satisfaction of work, and come to regard the only point of work as being a pay packet at the end of the week. And if they can obtain a pay packet without having to work for it, they risk terminal decline, since that situation can so easily be a breeding-ground for drugs and crime.

A further damaging spin-off to society comes from the destruction of worthwhile businesses as a result of crime, since assets worth millions are damaged or stolen, and insurance cover gives only short-term protection. This is because insurance claims inevitably lead to higher and higher insurance premiums, with incalculable damage to our economy.

That is my case for protecting the family unit. In the case of my own family I take both pride and pleasure in the fact that all my children appear to be happily married and have founded families for themselves. Furthermore, both they and their partners appear to have the happiness of job satisfaction. This above all is my memorial.

EPILOGUE

I have put together this life story over about fifteen years. When I started, I had been paying so many school fees that although 'half a million' seemed possible, it was by no means 'in the bag'.

Everyone says quite rightly that money isn't everything. But in this material world there are certainly many things you cannot do without it.

In my experience, people who decry money are very often the ones who expect other people to provide it for them. We live in a competitive world in which none of us is owed a living; and although we all expect to be justly treated, that cannot be guaranteed and should not be taken for granted.

At the very least, money can buy you and your family and your associates some comfort and a degree of security. It is also worth remembering that jobs are only created by the investment of capital, and that a major part of our lives is the work that we do.

On the whole, fortune has favoured us, and I am now reasonably secure having achieved financially more than I could reasonably have expected.

The fact remains that without Dorothy, the woman who has been my wife, the mother of my children and my life's partner in business matters, I could have done only a small fraction of what I have done.

Therefore I see no reason to change the title of this book from Half a Millionaire: because I am indeed Dorothy's 'other half'.

Pimley Manor, 1998